FROM THE
COUCH TO
THE KITCHEN

FROM THE COUCH TO THE KITCHEN (A BOOK TO INDULGE IN)

written by

The students of Dorsey High School

with a foreword by

Alice Waters

published by

826LA

Dorsey High School Student Editorial Board: Jamise Caesar,
Kendra Glover, Danae Mejia, Jalisa "Juju" Miller,
Joyce Realegeno, Rika R. Thibodeaux, Brian Young

Published April 2011 by 826LA

ISBN 978-1-934750-24-7

First Edition

826LA West   826LA East

685 W. Venice Boulevard   1714 W. Sunset Boulevard
Los Angeles, CA 90291   Los Angeles, CA 90026
310.305.8418   213.413.3388

http://826la.org

Design by Yello,Friends!
Pei-Jeane Chen, Patrick Leung, Carlo Llacar, Saejean Oh

Printed in Minnesota by Bang Printing

Distributed by PGW

This book was made possible by a generous grant from
the Goldhirsh Foundation.

THE PICNIC TABLE

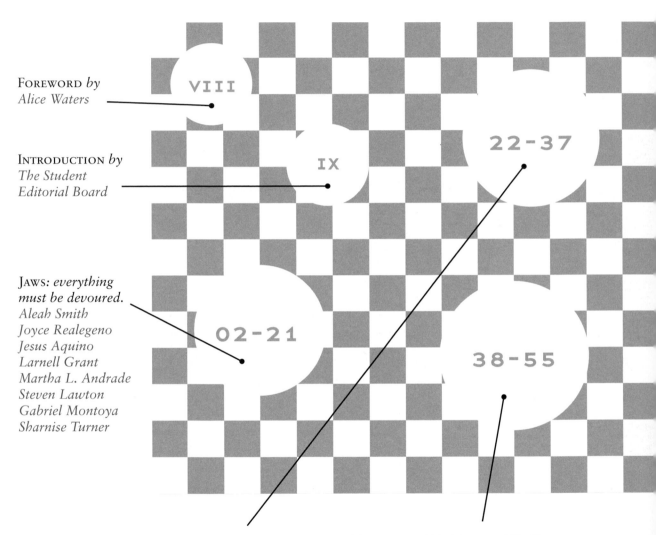

FOREWORD *by*
Alice Waters — VIII

INTRODUCTION *by*
The Student
Editorial Board — IX

JAWS: *everything*
must be devoured.
Aleah Smith
Joyce Realegeno
Jesus Aquino
Larnell Grant
Martha L. Andrade
Steven Lawton
Gabriel Montoya
Sharnise Turner — 02-21

22-37

38-55

FREELOADERISM: *sometimes things taste*
better when they require no more effort
than picking up your fork.
Symone Owens / Jessica Azucena Alberto
Franco / Marcos Durán / Ernesto
Rigoberto Panameno / Angie Lilibeth
Garcia / Engelle Valenzuela

TO GARDEN / TO MARKET / TO KITCHEN
Helen Elizabeth Garcia / Kevin O. Ruiz / Micheliza
Hernandez / Engelle Valenzuela / Priscilla Lira /
Raymond Villanueva / Brian Young

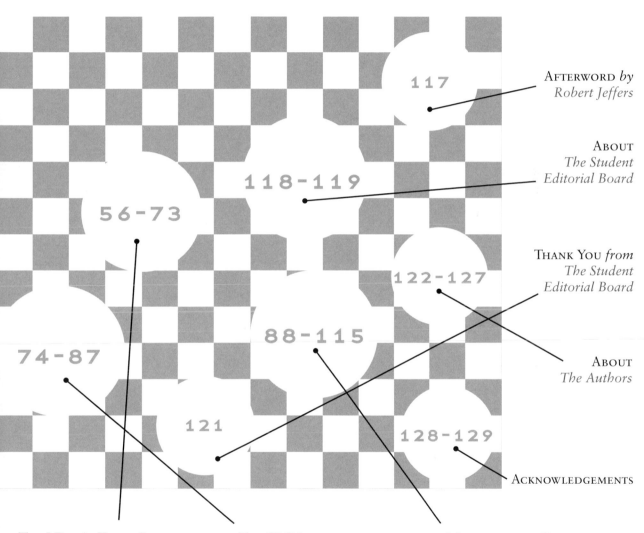

117 — AFTERWORD *by* *Robert Jeffers*

118-119 — ABOUT *The Student Editorial Board*

56-73

122-127 — THANK YOU *from* *The Student Editorial Board*

88-115

ABOUT *The Authors*

74-87

121

128-129

ACKNOWLEDGEMENTS

THE I-DON'T-KNOW BOWL:
mystery and adventure—pray the end product is edible.
Rika R. Thibodeaux / Jamise Caesar / Ivanna Rodriguez / Stephanie Overton / Gary Paul Burbridge III / Olga DeLeTorre / Marresha Milner / Blanca Reyes

THE BRC (BEANS, RICE, AND CHEESE) BURRITO:
not incredibly healthy, but intensely gratifying.
Kendra Glover / Jalisa Miller / Alysa R. Drew / Isaira Padilla / Dana Flores / Jasmine Littlejohn / Taylor Broom

MINGLING AND EATING
Irving W. Fuentes / Danae Mejia / Elizabeth Garcia / Jose Wilfredo Moran / Milan McKinney / Janet Nava / Jose Wilfredo Moran / Frederick Singleton / Yuisi Dennis / Luther Meriweather / Brian Young

Alice Waters

This collection of writing by students at Dorsey High School is an inspiring and soulful work. In these beautifully written narratives, the students describe their most personal experiences with food and the ways in which cooking and eating with their friends and families affects their lives. I began my restaurant as a way of gathering my friends together to enjoy a simple and delicious meal: these anecdotes perfectly exemplify the experience of community and togetherness I envisioned.

One student, Helen, tells of cooking her family's favorite meal of fried fish and rice, and describes the pleasure of serving the dish with a fresh salad made from her own vegetable garden. She shows us the beautiful continuity of creating a meal from beginning to end—from the vegetables planted in the garden to the family dinner table. Another student, Olga, conveys the inextricable link between food and family as she describes the group effort of preparing ceviche. Her brothers, sisters, and parents are each assigned a task in putting together the dish, from squeezing lemons to cutting vegetables to peeling shrimp. At the heart of Olga's tale is the joy of recreating a traditional recipe that has been part of her family for generations.

This project has encouraged students to sift through their memories, ultimately creating narratives with insight that will inspire readers of any age.

In a Nutshell— Some of us have known that we'd be making this book since the tenth grade. (Most of us are now in the eleventh.) Others just found out this year. We wrote, rewrote, and reconstructed our essays time and time again—Danae's piece has always been about yuca con chicharrón, while Jalisa's shifted from enchiladas to german chocolate cake. We spent a good amount of time working with 826LA tutors learning about the intricate process of writing. Besides composing our essays, we created illustrations with Miss Stacey to further personalize this book we call our own.

While there are many Dorsey students on this project, there are only seven of us who are on the editorial board. We helped decide on the cover, the design, and the order and organization of the pieces in this book together with 826LA, Mr. Jeffers, Miss Stacey, and the Yello,Friends! design team. Along the way, we learned that nothing is perfect the first time. We couldn't just sit around and do nothing; we learned that only through hard work and time spent would we be satisfied with the outcome. We took this opportunity and worked for months, and now we are seeing our "edible" work come together. (And, while working hard, some of us were able to try food that was completely foreign to us—some of us had never eaten organic produce, hummus, or gumbo before our editorial board meetings. Special thanks to you and your mom, Brian, for the gumbo!)

Hunger drives us all—hunger for sustenance, of course. But in a deeper sense, we are driven by hunger for companionship, hunger for adventure, hunger for space or solitude, hunger for memories, hunger for happiness…and all of these are part of the same primal hunger for satisfaction. Food quells this hunger and leads toward fulfillment. Food allows us to venture into a vault of experiences that we tend to ignore; it is a bridge that links us to a world that all too often escapes us.

This book is about food and the experiences it evokes—walking through a grocery store looking for the perfect pink chicken, remembering a beloved family member in apples and peanut butter, being reminded of a mother's unconditional love. This book is about appreciating our delectable experiences.

While delving into the worlds of the students who wrote these pieces, you might see a reflection of yourself—even though you may have never tried a pupusa or pizza with ranch drizzle over it. You'll still find that always-welcoming, always-comforting, always-heartwarming *ahhh* moment.

We invite you to get up from that couch, go into the kitchen, and indulge in this smorgasbord of stories.

(A BOOK TO INDULGE IN)

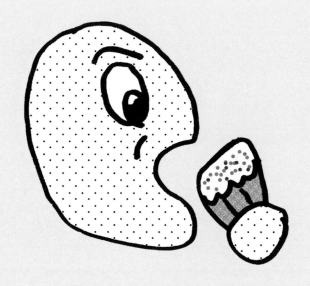

JAWS

Everything must be devoured.

ALEAH SMITH

It's Saturday morning, and I'm lying down in bed, watching *CSI: Miami*. I've already eaten breakfast, but I'm still hungry. Good thing my mom's going to make my favorite meal today. I just hope she doesn't ask me to—

"Leah! Get dressed! We're going to the grocery store in a few minutes."

Oh no...

I hate going anywhere on a comfortable Saturday morning. I'd rather eat, sleep, and watch TV. But I guess this time getting up is worth it since I'll get to eat my favorite meal later: steak served with yellow rice and cheese-covered steamed broccoli. My mom makes it a few times every month. She purchases the steak and other ingredients at Ralphs.

First, my mom chooses good quality steak—nice and thick chuck steak. We then go to the dairy section for the cheese. There are many varieties to choose from, but only one is perfect for the broccoli: cheddar! Some may like the broccoli with melted swiss or pepper jack cheese, but it's just not the same to me. Next, we go to the aisle with all of the grains, rice, and cereal. We always get Zatarain's yellow rice. It's a New Orleans–style food that was created in 1889. Chicken flavoring, molasses extract, and caramel coloring make the rice yellow. Its flavorful seasonings make my mouth water every time: salt, sugar, onions, bell pepper, garlic, chicken, and molasses.

The produce section is very colorful. Bright red apples, beautiful oranges, and so many green veggies! This is where Mom and I select the green and red bell peppers, onions, and cilantro for the steak. When picking the bell peppers, I look for ones that are ripe and have an even shape, meaning that they aren't all beat up or dented. I don't like the smell of the onions, especially when there are multiple onions in one area (because there the smell tends to be stronger). We select white onions or sometimes green onions for the steak. Either tastes great.

When selecting the cilantro, we prefer the bundle that's nice and green, not brown. Fresh food is the best food. We could also gather our broccoli here, but Mom always gets the frozen package of broccoli, which I think tastes as great as the hand-picked broccoli. I guess she finds it easier to buy the broccoli pre-chopped to save time in preparation.

After purchasing all of the fine ingredients, I lose all of my patience. Sometimes I even feel like running home with the groceries. All I see on the way back is home after home, tree after tree after home after tree—when will we be there?!

* * *

I hate this part about grocery shopping: where you come home and have to put away all of the groceries. All that's on my mind is food, food, and food! I rush every time my mom tells me to put away the groceries so that I can get comfortable afterward. My next move is to run to the kitchen to grab a snack while my mom prepares the meal. I eat something light that won't get in the way of my hunger, stuff like chips or sweet strawberries. The small snacks are just a tease and never last long.

In my room, watching TV and snacking, I can hear the water running from the kitchen sink. I like to think of it as a shower or bath for the vegetables. Then, chopping noises come from the kitchen. I can decipher each sound and know which vegetable my mom is chopping. The crunchy chop is the sound of an onion. The chop that sounds as though you're stepping on gravel is that of the cilantro. The bell pepper being chopped sounds like a watermelon being sliced open on a hot sunny day. I can hear her unwrapping the steak. She does it slowly when all I want her to do is speed up the process! The plastic makes an irritating noise; it sounds like it's screaming at my mom, telling her not to open the steak because it belongs in the package. Now she's seasoning the steak with all the noisy ingredients. Well…she takes her time with that, too. Then, finally! It feels good to hear the oven door opening and the pan hitting the oven rack. Time for that tasty yellow rice!

Now my mom's answering a phone call—*why is she answering a phone call?!* It only makes me wait longer and takes her mind off of cooking for a short while.

"Okay, bye."

Oh how sweet the sound of her ending that call! It's been three whole minutes, and I'm over here dying for this meal. The rice is boiling, the steak is baking, and now for the broccoli. The water for the broccoli is being boiled now, too. It sounds like a chemistry lab going on in the kitchen. Boiling water and broccoli are combined to create...steamed broccoli!

The meal is coming together now; I can smell it! My room is filled with the warm and pleasant aroma of everything wafting from the kitchen. I can almost taste it now. It's the last few minutes of preparation, but it feels like hours before I'll actually be able to enjoy the meal. It's making me more and more anxious as I think about it. I'm trying to be patient; it's almost here...

I can hear the oven door opening again. This time, food isn't going into it. The entire home is soaked in the smell of the food coming from the kitchen. You could leave the house and say hi to the neighbors, and they'd be able to smell it on your breath—and you haven't eaten any of it yet! I wait for my mom to call me into the kitchen. Seems like a mighty long time, Mom...when you gonna call me?

"Leah?!"

Yes! It's time! I jump out of my seat, tripping over my slippers, smiles and all. The wait is finally paying off.

I control myself when I enter the kitchen and stare at the wonderful creations from my mom's chemistry lab. I watch her place each portion onto my plate, lick my lips in awe, and lose my patience once more. The steam rises up to my face, teasing and taunting me with its nice scent and warm touch. I try to ignore it, but it's far too good. Only one more scoop to go.

My plate is full and the table is close. I stare at my plate on my way to the chair, and my eyes water as if they're sweating. They've been waiting pretty patiently for this, too. I'm seated and I've said grace. I don't even know where to start on this plate. Should I dig into the yellow rice? Take a few nibbles of the tender steak? Or should I eat some of the steamed, cheese-covered broccoli that's been hissing this whole time? Well, I guess I'll take a small portion of each one! My fork is on its way to my mouth. I don't hesitate at all because I recognize this heavenly taste. Its name is Mmmm and it comes from this Earth.

"Hi, Mmmm! You've met Tongue's buds before, haven't you?"

My mom enjoys this meal just as much as I do. But see, she's more patient than I. I don't know how she does it, but if I ever want to have this meal when I'm older, I sure won't think twice about making it on my own. It wouldn't even be the same if anyone else made it because it's a trademark of my mom's great cooking. She's made other tasty meals, but this one stands out the most. Now I understand why my mom took a year just to chop all of the vegetables and season the steak. You can't rush perfection. She takes her time to make it just right. The shopping and waiting were all worth it. This meal is the most exciting meal, I guess—the only one I'm ever impatient for, the one that befriended my tongue's buds with a warm greeting. The one I grew up eating.

I'm full now and fully satisfied.

"Thanks, Mom."

HUNGRY FOR COMFORT

JOYCE REALEGENO

After a stressful day at school (even after days that aren't stressful), there is nothing that I enjoy more than sitting on my bed, watching one of my favorite films, and eating one of my favorite foods—a Boca burger. Whether it be *Day of the Dead*, *The Thing*, or *The Shining*, my ritual would fail to be complete if the burger was not included.

From the time the bell rings for nutrition, anticipation of my afternoon meal has already begun to take shape. Throughout the school day, I keep my hunger in check with gulps of water and an occasional brownie. But once three o'clock comes along, I am well over my daily water intake and the sight of a chocolate treat makes my stomach churn. I race home as soon as the final bell rings. If I am incredibly deprived of both nutrition and energy, I will call my mom for a ride, but that doesn't happen too often. Walking home usually takes about twenty minutes. It's a little far from school, but why take the bus when you have legs, right?

Once I'm home, it is as if my brain goes on autopilot. I walk into my house and say hello to my mom and whoever else is home at the time. I go into my room, put my bag down, walk to the kitchen, and open the refrigerator. I grab the Boca burger box, and I begin cooking what is the most anticipated meal of the day. As the patty is simmering in the pan, I proceed to my room in search of a film to watch. It will most likely be either a horror film or one of the hilarious *Naked Gun* movies. Once I smell the patty starting to burn, I race back into the kitchen to flip it—by that time the bread is already toasted, and all of the remaining ingredients are ready to be applied to the burger.

Without cheese and barbecue sauce there would be no veggie burger. I can't explain why, but I love the combination of wheat bread, spinach, a veggie patty, barbecue sauce, tomatoes, and cheese. This incredibly simple meal (with a cup of orange juice on the side) and—of course—a great film are imperative not only to curb my appetite, but also to give myself a brief moment of comfort and relaxation before I indulge in a feast of textbooks and notes.

"Tengo hambre" (I'm hungry), I tell Mom as I walk to the refrigerator, pretending to look for something to make. I say *pretending* because I know I am not going to cook food on my own.

She slowly turns while making that annoyed face she always makes at my twelve-year-old brother Luis and me. She yells, "¡Cuando hay comida en la casa nunca quieres comer, y cuando no hay quieres comer!" (When there's food at home, you never want to eat, and there isn't food you want to eat!)

"He's just hungry," Dad says. "Why are you yelling?"

"Yo también tengo hambre" (I'm also hungry), Luis says, walking into the kitchen.

"Vamos a comer a Beto's Tacos" (Let's go eat at Beto's Tacos), Dad says, ending the conversation.

Beto's Tacos is six blocks away from where we live, and it is too close for driving. We actually enjoy walking because afternoons in my neighborhood are too nice to miss, and time with my family is actually a rare thing. Dad's always working, Mom's in the kitchen cooking, and Luis is playing video games on the computer.

At 6:34 my parents, Luis, and I leave the house, and we quickly turn onto Duray. We pass small streets as my parents walk side by side in front of Luis; I walk behind them. I always walk behind my family. I began doing this when I'd get in fights with the three of them. They say I like to argue a lot. It has become a habit to walk behind everyone now, and I have the space to think clearly.

As we slowly pass residential streets, I stare up at the sun setting in the fire-colored clouds. However, the smell of a full trash can thrown on the sidewalk ruins the moment because it distracts me from the scenery. The trash can contains rotting fruit and empty beer cans. I notice lots of cracks in the sidewalk, especially by a tree. These deep cracks look like tiny roads, all leading up to this tree that is trying to escape from the sidewalk; its roots are pushing upward through the cement.

I continue walking with my hands in my front jean pockets, and they become warm. My parents turn back to look at me, making sure that I haven't wandered off like I have in the past.

I see it, and suddenly stop. Only the heel of my right foot is on the ground now. I almost stepped on a snail, and the shadow of my shoe shades it. I back off a bit, bend down, and pull my right hand from my warm pocket to feel the shell of the shy snail.

I hop back up and continue walking the same streets that I've walked for the past three years. I see a patch of dandelions and pick one up. I stare at the seeds for a few seconds, and I blow on it. Only the stem is left, which I gently throw into the bush of red roses next to the dandelions. As I look up, I realize we are standing across the street from Beto's Tacos.

BITES OF SOUL FOOD

LARNELL GRANT

I love tasting everything on my plate. For my first bite, I go for the fried chicken. I love it because I taste the crispiness of the skin and the hot sensation of the meat. The first bite of the macaroni is good: you can taste the hot melted cheddar cheese. The greens are so hot and juicy, and they taste really good when they're hot. The first bite of the greens is the best because they cool down while you're eating everything else. The rolls are warm and tasty. The first bite, you just taste bread, but the second bite is the best because you can taste the butter a little better. Next, I take a sip of the Kool-Aid, and it's really tasty. After that, I take a second bite of the chicken, and it's still as hot and good as the first bite.

Oh yeah, I can't forget about the yams! That's my favorite part of the whole meal. The first bite of the yams is the best—they just have this unexplainable good taste. Once you put them in your mouth and they touch your tongue, your mouth lights up and your eyes open up wide. They put a smile on your face 'til your cheeks hurt. You're going to want more after you're done eating the yams. When I'm done eating, I get seconds, but not of everything. I get some more macaroni, greens, and yams, and after that I am stuffed.

I ALWAYS EAT THREE PUPUSAS

MARTHA L. ANDRADE

When I go to my friend's house, we talk about what we want to eat. We both agree on La Senasora, a Salvadoran restaurant. Her parents take us. When we enter, there are two big plasma TVs with a soccer game on. We sit down; the waitress asks if we are ready to order, and we say, "Yes we are!" My friend and I already know what we want to order, and that is three pupusas de revuelta. But as for her parents, they are still undecided on what they want to eat.

I always eat three pupusas because they're pretty big and it's the right amount that gets me full. Pupusas are round balls made out of masa (corn dough) with meat and cheese inside. Once they've put the filling in them, they flatten the ball of masa on the table and then lay it on a flat stove where they are cooked.

While our food is being cooked, we eat chips and salsa. When our food arrives, I get ready to eat. Her parents' meal looks really good, but I stick to my pupusas. I always get the pupusas that have a mixture of everything inside because I do not like eating just one thing, and that also goes for my friend. First, I put this topping on called repollo, which is a mixture of cabbage. Then I put on another sauce that's made of tomatoes. Both go really well with the pupusas. As for my friend, she eats them plain because she doesn't like the dressing or the sauce: she says she finds them nasty.

The way I enjoy my pupusas is eating them really quickly. I never use a fork and knife because I find it simpler to use my hands. But sometimes, when I rush to eat them right when they are served, I end up burning my lip because they are still really hot. I also love drinking iced tea with my pupusas, and I always ask for refills. My friend takes her time eating, and so do her parents because they have a lot of food on their plate. I end up waiting for them.

When I eat my favorite meal with my friend and her parents, we have so much to talk about because I don't really get to see her that often. We mostly talk about how she is doing and what she has been up to. I also talk to her parents. We laugh at jokes her dad makes. Sometimes we just make fun of each other, but we are just playing around.

Peaceful and Calm with Great Food and Service

Steven Lawton

My favorite restaurant would have to be Toast Bakery Cafe off of 3rd Street and Beverly. Toast appears to be upscale, with its fancy furnishings and overhanging eaves. The setting is very appealing to the eye, with calm colors and an open area. Many people like to eat outside, and I find it very peaceful to eat by the scenery next to the garden.

I normally go with my aunt. I don't know how we started going there, but now it seems like it's our religion to go on Sundays after church. Honestly, this is the only reason why I go to church. I don't know if you have ever been to a Catholic service, but can I just simply say, *BORING*? My aunt is into the church scene. She is always mad at me during service because she'll find me doing one of these things: texting in the restroom, sleeping on the bench, or buying something outside. That's my weekly church visit.

On our way to the restaurant, she asks me why I have no interest in church. The conversation always ends with me saying it's so boring. I'm growling, *Grrrrrrrrr,* which means I'm hungry. So as soon as we get there, I'm wondering, *Where in the heck is the food?* It is normally pretty busy, yet we have never waited for a table.

We walk up to the hostess, and she asks if we want Matt. Matt is always our server.

And we say, "Yeah."

Then she says, "You guys don't even need a menu, right?"

We shake our heads, no.

We go to Toast so often that Matt already knows what we like. I always start my meal off with a cup of pink grapefruit juice. It's normally sweet, but on days that it isn't, I add a packet of sugar. Then Matt comes over with my meal, the denver scramble. It's made of ham, onion, bell peppers, cheese, and egg. My aunt always gets something that looks nasty (healthy), like the protein scramble. It just looks disturbing. It appears wet, and the egg is covered in spinach, and then the turkey sausage is white, sort of like tofu. Then she always has the nerve to ask me if I want some!

If you want something sweet while you are there, most definitely get the Oreo banana pudding. It is so fluffy and creamy. The Oreos give it that smooth chocolate taste we all love. The pudding is very similar to ice cream—fluffy, and it melts in your mouth. The bananas are always fresh. Or you could get the Surprise Cake. When you see it, the first thought that comes to mind is, *Why is it blue? Something must have gone wrong with the batter.* It's cool; I thought the same thing. The Surprise Cake has food coloring in it, but it's just a regular white cake with blue frosting and sprinkles. It reminds me of a cupcake—very thick frosting but amazing after you take some of the excess off.

I would recommend Toast if you like a calm environment with great food and service. It isn't expensive, but you get quality food and a wide selection while feeling calm in an environment that is very hectic.

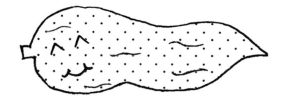

SALUTATIONS,
I AM SWEET POTATO...
DO NOT LET THE
NAME FOOL YOU!

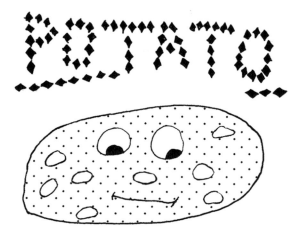

HI, MY NAME'S CASSAVA,
BUT PEOPLE CALL ME YUCA.

'SUP, I'M A SPUD.
I GREW UP IN MUD
AND I'M NOT A DUD.

CHOPPING

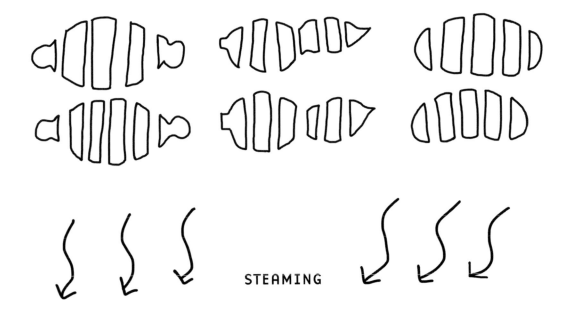

STEAMING

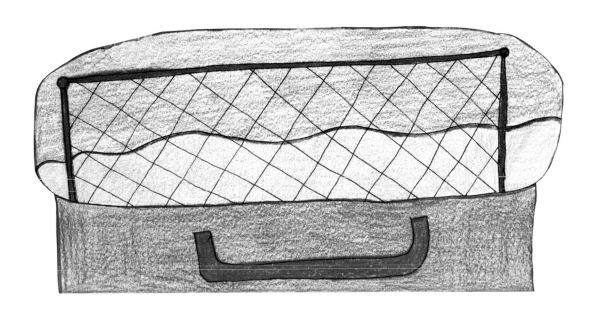

With Fireworks and Music

Gabriel Montoya

It's Saturday morning. I wake up around ten and go downstairs to watch TV. I hear a knock on the door, and it's my aunt and my uncle. They ask me if I want to go out with them, but they don't tell me where. I ask my mom if I can go, and she says yes. My cousins come as well, if they want to. If they do, we play around in the car before we start moving. I sit all the way in the back of the van with my cousin Aurora. My three little cousins, Bobby, Dina, and Nina, sit in the middle seats. My aunt drives, and my uncle sits next to her.

Once we start moving, everyone talks, but I am in my own world just looking at what's around us, wondering where we are going. I enjoy the view—the streets, the buildings, and even the people. I start to recognize some of these places and get happy once I know where we're going. I just can't wait. Aurora and I talk about what we are going to get. Our mouths get watery and our stomachs growl. When we arrive, I rush out of the car and wait in front of the restaurant until my family gets close. I open the door for them and wait 'til they all enter, and then I go in. I do that because that's the way I was raised.

* * *

Charly's is my favorite restaurant because they have great American and Mexican food. My family and I love this restaurant. We often go after we come back from the cemetery where we visit my grandpa. Or sometimes we just go to eat because we want Mexican food. It's twenty to thirty minutes away, located near Inglewood and Manchester. On days I know we're going, I like to rush the family into the car because I am just not patient.

There's not that much going on at the restaurant. On the walls, there are sombreros, guitars, and some picture frames. I like that it's not crowded because I don't really like being in a place with a lot of people. The restaurant is small. I can't really smell the food I like, but I can smell other types of food.

I like to get the wet burrito: a big burrito with rice, beans, and chopped beef inside; red salsa (not spicy) with melted cheese on top; and more beans and rice with a salad on the side. My family either gets a big bowl of nachos with cheese and jalapeños on top for everyone to share, or they get enchiladas, tacos, or cocktail shrimp for themselves.

It's an awesome place to hang out with the family. We spend our time there listening to music from the jukebox. You can play any kind of music you like; we mostly put on Spanish music. We enjoy talking about random stuff, mostly about our days, how we've been, and what we've been up to. My mom and my sister Jasmine mostly speak to each other in Spanish, and I just sit there pretending like I know what they are talking about. I don't know that much Spanish even though I am Latino; I mostly speak English.

When the food arrives in front of us, my stomach growls, my mouth gets watery, and my eyes get big. I drink some soda. I start by cutting the wet burrito down the middle. Then I cut it up into pieces and start munching on them one by one. Once I take a bite, it's like I'm going to a whole new world. Bite after bite is like a celebration in my mouth, with fireworks and music. I just have a big smile on my face. I get to the last piece, and the celebration starts to calm down until finally, it finishes.

I see myself back in the restaurant, sitting down at a table with an empty plate in front of me. Full, I just sit until my stomach gets better. And when that's happening, we're just talking again about our day or some stuff in the past, mostly funny stuff. We get up to leave and go home, but I wish I could go there more often. Sometimes I think I can walk from my house to the restaurant, but it's too far.

The front door was locked! I tried to stay calm as I watched my mother slowly gather her things from the car. It took her a whole three minutes to finally make it to the porch; it felt like hours. I think she took her time to get her keys out on purpose because she knew I was in a rush. She knows how agonizing it is to wait for her. She finally unlocked the door, and I almost knocked her down trying to get into the kitchen. I went right past my little brother crying on the floor. I walked right past my older brother and sister arguing. I didn't even speak to my dad. He always tells me to clean my room or fix up something as soon as I get in the house. Nope, not today! I wasn't going to let anything stop me from making my favorite snack.

Walking into an empty, quiet kitchen almost made me smile again. After I checked to make sure that no one was going to interrupt me and that I had all the materials I needed, I began the process of making my snack, starting with the apples. First I gathered two nice-sized, yellow apples from the bag. The apples I bought were perfect—juicy, round, fresh, and sweet! I pulled out the cutting board, grabbed a thin knife, and started slicing the apples evenly. Every time I prepare this snack, I cut the apples in half four times. Then I placed the slices onto a dry paper towel. Next I took out the peanut butter from the bag. The peanut butter was Jif—smooth, thick, creamy. I placed three spoonfuls of peanut butter into a bowl and put the bowl into the microwave for less than a minute. After the apples were nicely sliced and the peanut butter was smoothly melted, the snack was complete in less than five minutes. I could not wait to devour my peanut butter and apples!

START

FINISH!

FREELOADERISM

Sometimes things taste better when they require no more effort than picking up your fork.

Oxtail with Coconut Rice and Black Beans—Yum

SYMONE OWENS

My immediate family roots run as deep and as wide as a giant ficus tree, all the way down to Guatemala and Belize. Oxtail with coconut rice and black beans has been shared by my family, going all the way back to my great-great-grandmother. I love when my aunt makes this meal. The smell of the homemade dinner makes my mouth water and my stomach anxious. Often on Sundays, my family and I share this particular meal with sweet raspberry iced tea.

Usually when my aunt gathers the ingredients she drives to two different stores. Ralphs is the first stop, near La Brea and Rodeo. My aunt walks into the air-conditioned grocery store and heads into the pasta aisle where the jasmine rice is located. Her cabinets are always filled with dried beans and seasonings, so she never has to buy those two ingredients. The second store, Dat Moi, is in Gardena. My aunt walks over to the butcher and asks for five pounds of oxtail. While she waits, she goes to an aisle to get her favorite Marie Sharp's habanero pepper sauce. The wait for the oxtail takes only two minutes. After the scavenger hunt in both stores is over, my aunt heads home to start my favorite meal.

During the hour my aunt was shopping, my brother, cousins, and I were chopping the red bell peppers, onions, garlic, cilantro, and green onions. When my aunt gets home, she washes her hands and gets into the process of cleaning the oxtail. She throws seasoning and vegetables from every direction into the bowl with the oxtail. Everyone's faces light up when the oxtail is then thrown into the pot to simmer and stew. To make the rice and beans, my aunt boils seven cups of the jasmine rice with half a pot of water and a full can of coconut milk. We can't forget the drained canned black beans! While everyone patiently waits for the food to be done, we sit around the living room in front of the TV to watch movies galore, from *Rush Hour* to *Welcome Home*, Roscoe Jenkins.

Movies that have humor are our ultimate favorites. We all laugh our heads off to Martin Lawrence and Chris Tucker. The fabulous aroma of the meal begins to get heavier and heavier. My aunt gets up to check and see if the food is ready. Two minutes later my aunt starts chanting, "The food is readddy, guys, the fooood is ready. Come and eat!"

We race over to dish our food quickly. We've waited so long to finally eat the savory oxtail with white coconut rice and black beans. The tender well-cooked meat falls off the bone and never gets stuck between my teeth. The mixed seasonings and herbs—black pepper, pollo (chicken flavor seasoning), oregano, onion powder, garlic powder, and parsley—bring an unexplainable tremendous flavor that would cause tears to roll off an angel's cheek. The rice and beans are just right, not too hard or soft, fully firm. The tropical flavor of coconut milk brings joy to my face and has my taste buds jumping. This dish brings the family together. I couldn't ask for anything more when my aunt makes my favorite meal. Although I despise washing sky-high dishes by myself, I don't complain because it's my turn every Sunday. Oh well! I had my satisfaction, and that's the love of my favorite meal. Family dinners are my favorite because we can go back for thirds. I mean, who can go back for thirds when they're eating their favorite meal? Everyone gets full and lazy. That usually happens when you eat a pretty large meal.

My grandmother often suggests that my mom should consider getting me a passport so that I can meet a few of my family members. Honestly I couldn't care less about learning Spanish; I just want to eat the varieties of food. My mom just thinks about the cost, not the valuable lessons and experiences I can consume while on the trip. When I lived in the Bronx, my cousins showed me pictures of themselves on the beach with their feet in the sand. Often, they would go to Guatemala during the humid season, the spring, for break. Faithfully, they wore chancletas (flip-flops), shorts, and T-shirts. My cousin Beverly bragged about how she learned Spanish in two-and-a-half weeks, but I wasn't really concerned about that: my mind

was just on the food. We were skimming through the pictures for a couple of minutes, and I saw a picture of my aunt eating coconut rice and black beans with stewed oxtail! My stomach began to thunderously growl. Beverly laughed loudly and called me greedy. She knows how much I love to eat, especially stewed oxtail with coconut rice and black beans.

OCHA!

JESSICA AZUCENA
ALBERTO FRANCO

OCHA! It's my favorite restaurant. It has the best food I've ever had, and everyone who has had the Ocha soup can agree with me. Since I was a one-year-old, I have been going to this place where my family, cousins, aunties, and uncles get together to catch up, talk, laugh, and enjoy each other's company. I really don't even have to try to get there: if we are in the car and we are hungry, we go! We always end up going at night. That's the best time to go. When we arrive, I can't wait to get out of the car. I'm looking out the window, seeing if Ocha is full; I don't like to wait in line. They still have to look for tables together when we show up because we aren't a small family.

Yes! We get our table. My mom asks her brothers what they would like. I never order the food; my mom usually orders for all of us. I don't even have to look at the menu because I already know what I want: shrimp soup, white rice, egg rice, noodles, beef with broccoli, and iced tea to drink. That iced tea is bomb; I want to get the recipe. It tastes like orange but with a creamy ice-cold topping. It's like a cold dessert. Doesn't it make your mouth water? Once again, I have to wait for the food to come to my table, but not for too long. They move pretty fast. I can hear the plates hitting against each other. It's so busy all around me! I can see the steam coming out of the kitchen. It smells so good. It's a limy smell that makes my tummy twist. Seeing the people around me starting to eat, I just want to get up and ask them, "Are you gonna eat that?" But I won't because I can't wait to get my hands on my own food.

When I see the waiters with plates of food, I'm hoping they're mine. If they pass my table, I'm bummed, and I start playing around with my plates and silverware. Then I see drinks coming. I know they're ours because we ordered a bunch of iced tea and, as always, one soda for my stepdad. When drinks are done with, now I know my food is on the way; I can already smell it. Next, they come out with the soups. They put one on each side and another in the center. I can see everyone looking at the food with smiles and hunger. I know they're hungry because I know I am! They must be! The waiter gets a match from the pack and drops it in the center of the soup. There's an empty place in the middle of the bowl to put the flame in so that the soup stays warm for you. It is very classy. Then, they bring out the other plates to complete our order.

I put the white rice in my bowl really quietly. I am usually the first one to get some soup. I love this soup! When it's on my table already, I can't wait. I pick up the spoon, dip it into the bowl, grab a mushroom, look at it, and just rush it into my mouth. Everything around me is no longer there. I lose myself. I am alone, just my shrimp soup and me. I taste the citrus. The mushroom sucks in some of the limy flavor. I always get seconds when I am halfway full, but not until I have had some egg rice with shrimp, and the beef with broccoli. That's the last part of my meal. I push the bowl to the side, get my plate, get my fork, grab the noodles, and drop them onto my plate; then I ask for the plate of rice. I take a spoon to get my rice with eggs, dip the spoon, and grab again. I can't get beef with broccoli! It's all gone! Oh well, I am going to get full anyway. I drink a sip of my iced tea, then another. The taste is so different from other drinks; it can't be found anywhere but Ocha.

I twist my noodles onto my fork, pull up, and put them into my mouth. I am trying to eat nicely and not suck the noodles. It's not ladylike. I feel like people around me are looking. I get shy, so I put my hand by my mouth—I don't want people seeing all of that. Then I start to munch on my food, fast, because it's so good all together. Then I start slowing down—slower and slower. That lets me know that I am full. I can't eat anymore. I am going to blow up! I feel like a fat cow. My jeans are too tight. I unbutton my jeans and pull my shirt over them so no one will ever know. It is my little secret, but I know my mom does it, too, even though I don't see her. I got it from her!

Everything I am doing now feels so slow. I just lie back in my chair letting the food go down. I can hear everyone talking, but I don't pay any attention. I am too full to listen and too lazy to move my mouth to talk. I feel so weak. I pick up my drink and sip it through my straw slowly, sipping to the last drop. I hear my mom order an extra iced tea. I am looking at her with wide eyes and a smile. She knows I want it; I am full, but I have to have it. They pass it to me, and I see my tía spotting my iced tea with the same eyes I gave my mom. So I ask her, "You want some?" She says, "Yeah, pass it on." So I share it with her. I don't think I can finish it by myself anyway. Meanwhile, when we are waiting for the check to come, they give us candy! We get the check, and we pass the candy around so that everyone gets one. I ask my mom for a dollar because they sell some sweet sugar candy. It's called tamardo. It's in a little box. I have to have my sweets after dinner. Everyone gets up, and we walk out the door. It's dark outside; I didn't even notice that it was night already.

Christmas Morning

Marcos Durán

My favorite food is my mom's tamales. The reason I like them is because she makes them only on Christmas and I must wait until Christmas to eat them.

When I wake up on Christmas, the first thing I smell is the tamales. That smell always reminds me of Christmas morning. My mom always made tamales on Christmas, so when I smell them, it reminds me of being a little kid. My mom's tamales make me feel happy.

Nobody makes tamales better than my mom. My mom's

tamales are not spicy, and that is why they are different from other people's. Most everyone tries to make them spicy because a lot of people like them that way. My mom makes three different kinds of tamales: pork, chicken, and cheese. My favorite tamales are the pork and the chicken, but I don't like the cheese. My older brother likes all tamales. My mom likes them all, and my dad only likes pork. My little brother likes the chicken and the pork, and my two little sisters like chicken and pork too. The first to go are the cheese because my mom makes only a few, then the pork. The chicken tamales are the last to go because we run out of the rest. All of the tamales are gone in three days.

On December 23, my family and I go to the store. We head north on Ferndale toward Rimpau, take the third left onto La Brea, turn left at Manchester, and turn right at Prairie. The store is on the left side of the street. While we are there, my mom buys all the materials that we need to make the tamales: flour, meat, and chili.

The next morning my mom starts to make the tamales. She starts making them in the early morning, and it takes until the end of the day. My mom cooks the tamales in a big pan that can fit lots of tamales. I don't know how she makes them because I am sleeping or watching a movie like *The Godfather* because it is one of my favorites. Then my brother and I play games to pass the time before Christmas.

On Christmas morning, we wake up, then start to open our gifts. This is fun because we see what our parents got us, and then our parents see us use their gifts. It makes them happy when we like our gifts. And after we have finished opening gifts, we start to eat the tamales.

On Christmas the food is so good. The tamales are soft. When you take a bite, you don't have to use a lot of force. The meat and the chili inside the tamales have the flavor of Christmas for me. It is usually cold, or maybe raining, so my mom makes hot coffee to drink with the tamales.

We are out of school, and my dad is not working. My mom is a good cook, and we eat all day. Everyone likes to eat the tamales in their own time and place. My dad and mom both like eating in the kitchen, and my sisters like eating in their room. My brothers and I eat in our room while watching the game or something on TV, maybe with the Los Angeles Lakers or the Orlando Magic. I eat a lot of tamales, and I don't stop until I feel sick. After the game, I go help my mom clean up because I like to help out, and we clean the house because it is dirty. Then I go eat for the third time.

The reason I like Christmas is not the gifts—it is eating my mom's homemade tamales.

CHOOSE YOUR BREAD   CHICKEN
OR
HAM?   WHAT CHEESE?

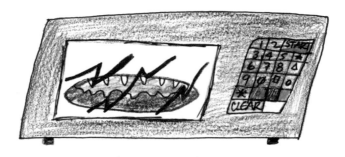

MICROWAVE OVEN

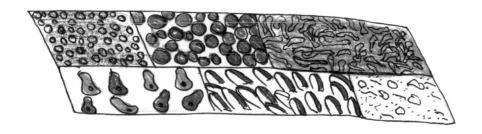

CHOOSE WISELY!

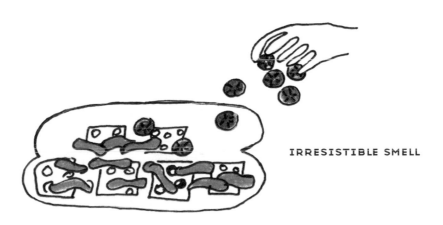

IRRESISTIBLE SMELL

ERNESTO RIGOBERTO
PANAMENO

On a warm summer night around eight, right after church, my family and some very close friends of ours chose to go out to a restaurant. We were in the lonely church parking lot that had a cold, hard, black floor when we finally came to a decision on where we wanted to eat. It was Olive Garden. We went to the Olive Garden in Glendale, which is about ten minutes away from the Glendale Galleria. On the way to the restaurant, we took the freeway. It was moving pretty fast. It took us about thirty-five minutes to arrive at the restaurant.

The first step we took into the restaurant, we could feel the warm air from the heater. The waiting time for us to get seated was about twenty-five minutes, so we decided to wait out on the cold seats around the fountain. This fountain was gray and very hard. Inside the fountain was a blue floor with a white wall surrounding it. While we were sitting down waiting, I decided to touch the water. Leaning to touch the water, I saw that it was clear and that there were a lot of coins at the bottom of the fountain. When the tip of my finger touched the water, I felt very cold. I felt a rush all over my body, like I was being frozen, and it started from the tip of my warm, soft, beautiful finger.

The waiting time was over. We went back inside the warm restaurant. A cute, beautiful, blond waiter seated us in the middle of the restaurant. The table that we were seated at was very different from the other tables. Our table was rectangular, and all the other tables were round. The seats were light brown with red, padded bottoms. They were very comfortable and relaxing. The waiter asked us for our drink order. I ordered a strawberry mango virgin margarita. While we were waiting for our drinks, we had a nice conversation about when I was small and the things I did, but when the drinks, the bread, and the salad came, everyone sat, quiet. I have to admit, every time I see warm baked bread with a little bit of cheese on top, my mouth waters, and it drives my taste buds crazy. The salad always looks fresh: very green and very juicy. The waiter asked us if we wanted cheese on our salad, and I said, "Yes, please," with a nice smile on my face. The strawberry mango margarita was red with a blend of yellow. It was cold and sweet.

I was the first one to dig into the fresh, juicy salad. I served myself and my little brother, too. The salad was delicious. It tasted like the salad was made from God's garden. Like always, every bite I took was as good as the last one. I looked at everyone's face, and they looked happy and satisfied. When we finished our first batch of bread, I asked for more because I like to eat it with the pasta. The waiter just looked at me and grinned. When the main dishes arrived, they looked so good! They also looked hot—you could see little bits of steam coming from the pasta. The pasta that I ordered is called chicken alfredo. I picked up the cold, silver fork and dug right into the delicious dish. The first bite was delicious, but the next bite was even better. What I liked about my pasta was that it had chicken, and I love chicken, especially when it is marinated with alfredo sauce. Everyone was having a wonderful time, but nobody enjoyed their pasta like I did. Then the waiter came by to leave the check, bringing chocolates with mint in them. They were good.

Olive Garden is my favorite place to go eat. Why? Because I spend time with my family and friends, and it's also a good environment for the family. The food is great, too. When I leave Olive Garden, it makes me want to eat there more often because they make you feel like you're at home. The design of the restaurant is like the inside of a European house, so if you aren't at home and you want to feel at home, you can always visit Olive Garden.

Panda Express: My Addiction

Angie Lilibeth Garcia

My favorite food is from Panda Express. I love it so much that I once ate it for breakfast. My family was going to Sacramento—a six-hour drive from Los Angeles—and we had to wake up at three in the morning to get there by nine. We had been on the freeway for five hours, and we were all tired, squished, and uncomfortable, so we decided to stop at a gas station. We got out for a stretch, and my mom asked me if I wanted to eat something.

"Yeah! I want Panda Express!" I said.

My mom annoyingly started up, "Oh my God! Here we go again! You tell me you don't get bored eating it all the time, and now you're asking to go there again!"

"Nope! Never!" I confidently replied.

She then conceded with defeat in her voice, "Fine. Let's go buy it. But don't come crying to me when your stomach starts hurting!" With a dose of teenage confidence, I happily accepted her offer.

When we got to Panda Express, I ordered—like always—spicy chicken, orange chicken, chow mein, and fried rice. My favorite is the spicy chicken. It's a spicy stir-fry with crunchy peanuts, diced red bell peppers, and sliced zucchini. The chow mein is whole grain noodles tossed with green onions, celery, cabbage, and bean sprouts. I love the taste of this. The fried rice is prepared by tossing and frying steamed rice with soy sauce, scrambled eggs, green peas, carrots, and green onions. And the orange chicken just has orange sauce that gives the chicken a sweet-and-spicy flavor.

I *never* get bored of this meal. Its flavor is so good and so unique that you'll never stop and think, *Hmm, this tastes like this other kind of food.* Oh, no. Never.

My love for Panda Express started when my mom once asked me what I wanted to eat. At first I didn't know, but I then decided on Chinese food.

"It doesn't matter where you get it from," I said. She

quickly left to buy it and later came back with the food and gave it to me.

As I took my first bite I said, "Oh my God. This is *so* good. Where did you get this from?"

"I was passing by to see if I could find any Chinese food, and I saw a restaurant called Panda Express. I went in and saw there was Chinese food, so I went to go order," she said.

I thought the food was good, but I didn't start loving Panda Express at that moment. It took a while because that was my first time tasting this kind of Chinese food. It tastes different from other Chinese food I had eaten—*really* different.

I now usually go to Panda Express with my auntie. She always takes me out to eat, so she already knows what I want to get—she doesn't even have to ask me. She knows I am going to say Panda Express. We always end up getting food at two different places so my auntie doesn't have to eat what I want to eat.

We go to Fox Hills Mall every weekend—not for the shopping, but for the food. In fact, we won't start looking around until we're done eating. Once we get our food, my auntie always wants to eat at a table that's at the edge of the food court, where you can see the whole mall. We like to look at the people walk back and forth in all different directions. I like spending time with her because she's not only fun, but she also buys me things.

But always—and much like my mother—my auntie asks me if I ever get bored eating Panda Express all the time.

"*No*. Why do you even ask me if you know the answer to that question?" I'll reply, annoyed.

"I get bored just seeing you eat it," she replies. I just laugh, not caring about what she is telling me. My mom tells me that when you call something "your drug," it's a way of expressing your addiction to something you really like. Panda Express is my addiction. I just *love* it.

Like Abracadabra

Engelle Valenzuela

Gumbo fills the whole room with its delicious, meaty, seafood-like smell. I cannot wait for that first spoonful of gumbo to hit my taste buds and take me into the delightful sensation I was longing for. I walk to the kitchen, where I take my first bowl of gumbo and grab a nice, crisp Sprite from the refrigerator. If I am going to eat gumbo, then I have to prepare the meal to my satisfaction.

I walk to the sink to wash off the top of the soda can, the way I was taught to do when I was little, because who knows what kind of germs lurk there. I crack open the soda, and a whiff of the famous lemon-lime smell runs across my nose. I cannot take it any longer—I have to sit down and eat.

Typically, one may think that it is normal and appropriate to sit down and share a delicious meal with your family members while talking about your day. I agree with that—sometimes. But sometimes a meal tastes better when you are so wrapped up in it that the outside world does not exist anymore. Sometimes you just want to be alone and not have anyone bother you while you are captivated by your meal. Have you ever heard that phrase from Carl's Jr., "Don't bother me; I'm eating"? Well, when I am eating gumbo, this very much applies.

When my grandmother makes gumbo, it is not a family meal. It's more like grab-and-go. I go back to my same spot on the couch, and my Sprite and gumbo are there to accompany me. The television is on, of course. I always say that food tastes better when you are watching TV. The best television show to watch while eating gumbo has to be a comedy or drama, or maybe even both combined. I love to watch MTV because it does not matter what show or movie you are watching; you will always be captivated by the amount of drama and comedy that that show has. It's only normal to watch television while you are eating, right? Or am I the only one who does so? Anyway, I have the gumbo (check) and the soda (check). I have to make sure the meal is just right before I eat it. Then, I waste no time and start to devour it.

I drink some of the soda to wet my throat, and then I eat

a combination of foods. I love the fluffiness of the rice and the juiciness of the sausages, and although most people do not like the slime of okra, I think that is one of the best parts. I take a spoonful of all that delicious goodness, including some of the flavorful stew, and when it all hits my tongue at once, it sends me into a food frenzy. I have a method to eating; sometimes, I eat things so as to specifically save the best-tasting ingredient for last. When I finish devouring the gumbo, there lies the crab. I waste no time cracking it open. I start by sucking the juice out, and I taste the juice of the gumbo and the crab flavor. Then I take out the crab meat, and I devour that as well.

When I eat gumbo, it is like *abracadabra*, the food suddenly disappears. I rush back to the kitchen for more, and luckily I get there in time to have seconds. But this time I don't get a big piece of crab, given that crab is expensive and there has to be enough for everybody. I start my eating process all over again, and sadly, when I am done, there will not be thirds left to eat.

TOMATO

CABBAGE

ONIONS

LETTUCE

TO GARDEN/
TO MARKET/
TO KITCHEN

HELEN ELIZABETH GARCIA

I was walking down my block and saw so many flowers. To my left was a nice garden. All the veggies and fruits were ready to eat. I opened the gate and was walking toward the garden when I saw an old man coming out from the side door of his house. When he saw me, he screamed, asking what I was doing on his property. I ran and slammed into a wall I didn't see. And then I woke up in my bedroom and saw that everyone was asleep. It was only a dream.

I put my pillow to my face and thought, *How weird*. First I was dreaming of flowers because I know I love flowers, but then it was all about veggies and fruits…well, kind of. I just left that thought aside and went back to sleep.

When I woke up in the morning and went to the kitchen, everybody was eating breakfast. I went back to my room, got clothes, and went to take a shower. After I finished with every-thing, I went to the kitchen and got a drink of orange juice.

I asked my mother if I could go to the park to take a walk.

She said, "Sure. Just be careful."

I said, "Okay, then."

As I was walking out the door, my little niece ran to me, and I asked her if she wanted to come. She said yes, so I went back in and told my mother that I was taking Marian.

She said, "Okay, just take care of her."

I got her little bag and put some snacks in (grapes, apple juice, and a little bag of cookies), and then we took her scooter and left.

As I was walking with my niece, I looked around the neighborhood and saw colorful houses of different shapes and sizes, old and new. I saw a lot of trees, too, and cars. They all looked weird in a nice way because there were new cars, old cars, faded cars, even crashed cars.

When Marian and I got to the park, she ran to the swings and told me to push her, and then she told me that she wanted to go on the slide. After a while, she got tired and said that she was thirsty and hungry. I got her bag, and she ate her grapes and cookies, then drank her apple juice. After that, we just lay in the grass and looked at the clouds for half an hour. I looked at my iPod and saw it was two o'clock. I told her that we needed to go back home. She sat down and made a face, saying no and crossing her two little arms across her little chest. I told her that we were going to be back next week, but for now we had to go home or Mommy wasn't going to let us come to the park again.

She said, "Okay then. Let's go home."

So I packed up everything I had brought and took her hand. As we walked back home, I told her, "Let's play a game. The game is I spy. You go first."

"Okay. I spy with my little eye a little cute thing."

I thought for a second and asked, "Is it you?"

She said, "*Nooo* silly-willy! It's that little puppy asleep on that chair."

I looked to my right and saw the puppy. The front porch was all dirty, and the lawn had big holes and was full of dog toys and kid's toys. The flowers and bushes were all messed up, too. Everything looked bad.

"Okay," I said. "Now it's my turn." I looked around and saw two little birds in a nest on a tree, with two baby birds. "I spy with my little eye two animals that can fly, with two babies, and they're on something high. The colors are green and brown."

She looked around, then pointed at the birds in the tree, and I just nodded my head yes. We played the game all the way home. When we got there, we saw that everyone was watching a movie and eating sandwiches. I told my little niece to go get washed up for lunch, and after I made her a sandwich, we sat down and watched the movie.

The next day I made breakfast for everyone. As usual, I made pancakes, eggs, sausages, orange juice, and coffee. When everything was ready, I woke everyone up. My father had a hard time trying to wake up because he came home at two in the morning from work. By the time he woke up, everybody was eating at the table. We all saw he was tired and still sleepy, and we all said good morning. He said good morning back, sat down, and started eating. I finished last, like always (I'm a slow eater), so I washed the dishes while my sisters cleaned the kitchen. After we finished, I cleaned the living room, my little sister did the bathroom, and my older sister did the bedroom.

After we were done, I went to my room. The shelf beside my bed was a mess, so I took everything off and cleaned it. I looked through my things and saw a book that I'd never read. The color of the book caught my eye, so I left it out and kept on fixing my things. Then I finished a book that I had started on Monday, took a shower, and went to sleep.

The next morning, I woke up and stayed in bed watching TV. The little ones came running in to hug me and to tell me that breakfast was ready. We ate the usual eggs, pancakes, etc. After I helped clean up, I went back to my room, sat down on my bed, and thought about what to do: should I draw, read, listen to music? Then I remembered that I had that book. I found it on top of the other book that I had just finished, and I started reading.

I liked the book. It had lots of colorful flowers. I was so amazed at how many types of flowers there are in the world. There are some that have venom, some that smell like candy, and some that are really sweet, but the thing that I loved the most was the colors. There were so many colors. I saw colors that I didn't even know were colors. I loved the roses, too. I loved everything in this book…I went to sleep, and the next morning I woke up to read it again, and I read for the rest of the afternoon.

One day after I finished reading the book about plants, I went to my backyard and smelled the red and white roses. They had a sweet, nice scent, and the tops felt kind of wet and soft. I even heard some bees in the roses. I picked one red and one white rose, and then I went into my house, found something to put them in, and put them on my lamp table. After that, I went to the store and bought seeds, then went home to start a garden. I made little holes in the dirt, dropped seeds in the holes, covered them with dirt, and watered them.

Days passed. I bought plant food and kept watering the seeds. One morning, I woke up, made breakfast for everybody, cleaned around the house, and then went outside to check them. The outdoors felt fresh and good. It wasn't hot or cold; it felt just right. As I looked around the corner, I saw little sprouts in rows on the ground. I ran to see them. They looked so tiny. I watered them and kept them away from little creatures and kept them nice.

Days became weeks, weeks became months, and before I knew it, I saw them fully grown.

One day I was cooking dinner for the family. It rarely happens, but my father was home at last for dinner. I made their favorite—fried fish and rice—and on a separate plate I put a salad made from the veggies from my garden. I made lemonade, too. I put the plate of food on the table with the plate of veggies. The little ones made faces, but I told them they should try something before making a nasty face.

"Marian," I said, "Do you want to try? It's really good, and plus, I have a good dessert for everybody too."

She thought about it for a while, and then she said, "Okay." She tried some and said, "Mmm, this is really good, Tía Helen."

I said, "Really?"

And she said, "Yes."

She had even more. A little while later they all tried some. They even wanted seconds. I was so proud of myself. They all thanked me for the food. I said that it was no problem and that it was my pleasure to cook for them.

My sisters helped me clean the table and wash the dishes. Then I started to get nine plates so I could serve dessert. I asked if anybody wanted fruit salad, and everybody said, "Me!" at the same time and laughed.

I gave some to my mother, my niece, my nephew, and my older brother. My older sister gave some to my father, my little sister, and my baby nephew. Then my sister and I got some for

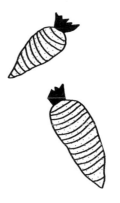

each other. We went to the living room, where we all watched a Tyler Perry movie: *Madea Goes to Jail*.

I had fun making all of that food for them, and I felt like they went to bed happy. I felt proud of myself because they all loved the food. The day was great, and I felt that this should happen every day, and that everything should always be this perfect.

THE JOURNEY FOR BARBECUE CHICKEN

KEVIN O. RUIZ

It's seven o'clock, and my family and I are sitting in the living room watching a movie. My big brother Gustavo brings up food, and everyone starts to get hungry, so we start discussing what we want to eat. I bring up barbecue chicken, and surprisingly everyone agrees with me. My sister Jennifer, my sister-in-law Maria, and I get on YouTube to find out what ingredients we need and how to make barbecue chicken. We make a small checklist: chicken, barbecue sauce, and our choice of rice.

We walk out the front door of our apartment complex, make a right on La Brea and Exposition, and keep walking until we get to the light on La Brea and Rodeo. After that, we make a left to cross the light toward Del Taco, and then a right to cross the other light toward McDonald's. Then, we walk straight until we get to Ralphs. As I walk into the market, I feel the cold air on my face and smell the floor wax. Every time we go to the store, we always get more than what we came for, so I get a cart first.

As we walk down to get the rice, we see some sodas and remember that we don't have anything to drink. Most of the time we get Coca-Cola whenever they have it, so we pick up a twelve-pack. Then we go for the barbecue sauce. We usually get sweet-and-spicy because my family likes spicy food, but since there are kids in the house, it can't be too spicy. After we get that, we go for the chicken legs. We get legs because they are easy to hold and taste good. As we get in line to pay, I remember that we need to get some water for my mom because she doesn't drink soda, so I go and get it. When I make it back to the cash register, I see that Jennifer and Maria have already paid and are waiting for me. I get back in line and am about two customers behind, so I have to wait, but I finally pay and we go.

We leave Ralphs and start walking home, but when we cross the street, we get a phone call from Gustavo. He tells us that he wants some chips, so we walk into CVS and get Hot Cheetos. Gustavo likes them because he really likes spicy foods. We start to walk home again, and I see some friends of mine and stop to say hello. But Jenny and Maria are rushing me, so I just wave. We keep walking, and Jennifer sees some of her friends. To get back at her, Maria and I tell her to hurry up, and we keep walking.

When we make it home, the first thing I do is put the sodas in the freezer to get cold before we start eating. I give Maria the barbecue sauce, the chicken, and the rice because she is cooking that day. But then my sister-in-law realizes that she needs brown sugar, and she sends me to go and get it. So I go back, and since I am running, all I really see is the sidewalk and some stores. I make it to Ralphs and get the brown sugar, then start to run home. There, I see my dad pulling up from work and parking, so I go say hi. Because I look tired, he asks me where I went, and I tell him that Maria needed brown sugar. "Did you get the right one?" he asks. I tell him, "Yes, I think." We walk in from the parking lot, and right when I walk in the door, Maria tells me that we had the brown sugar in the cupboard the whole time. So that's not cool, but at least we now have enough for the next time, so it's okay.

I'm not really sure how to make barbecue chicken, but I think you first pour the seasoning over the chicken, and then you boil it. After it's boiled, you pour a mix of brown sugar and barbecue sauce on the chicken, and then you put the tray of chicken in the oven. When it's all done, the food looks so good and tasty. It looks steamy because it's right out of the oven and really juicy because of all the barbecue sauce. I really love barbecue sauce, but I can't just eat; I have to wait for everyone else. I'm lucky because the smell is going around the house, and everyone starts to come.

Finally we start to eat. My first bite is so good, but I'm thinking that maybe I should slow down and try to enjoy my food for once. So I slow down, and that helps a lot because I get full and can't finish. Usually I would get seconds, but now I put some away for later, if I get hungry.

Nowadays, Maria cooks barbecue chicken more often. Usually after I'm done, I feel relaxed and a little sleepy, but the night's not over yet. When everyone is done eating, the family either plays a board game or plays with my cat Midnight, whom we've had since she was born about eleven months ago. Since then she has grown a lot, but that's another story.

Let's Go Eat Pizza!

Micheliza Hernandez

My story begins in the state of New Jersey. I went two summers ago. It was my first time going to New Jersey, and I was excited—I wondered what it was going to look like. My cousin and my aunt took me around, and I noticed there were bridges everywhere.

One day when we had nothing to do, my cousin asked me, "What are you down to eat today, Mich?"

"I don't know, anything," I answered. Then I added, "Wait, let's go eat pizza!"

My aunt butted in, saying, "Let's take her to the best pizza in town!"

All three of us agreed to go. My aunt lives on the fourth floor, which is the top floor of her building. I was stoked, but not so much about the whole walking-down-the-stairs thing. God, I really didn't want to walk down those stairs, but I was hungry. Then my aunt screamed in Spanish, "¡Vámonos, güeras!" (Let's go, chicks!) So we rushed to finish fixing ourselves up. When we were ready, we walked down the hellish road, the stairs.

After walking downstairs, we got into my aunt's car, a black, four-door Toyota Corolla that was parked in front of the Chinese restaurant at the bottom of her building. When my aunt started driving, we came across some traffic. I took advantage of the whole traffic situation to take a look at my surroundings. Looking left then right, I saw buildings, restaurants, and a fancy diner, although the one store that really caught my attention was Dunkin' Donuts. There was a Dunkin' Donuts on almost every street we passed.

After all that wonder, we came upon a small street. On the corner of the street was a pizza place with an average-size sign that said "Carmine's Pizzeria" in big, bold letters. Right next to the pizzeria was a hair salon. There was a lot of litter on that corner—crushed Coca-Cola cans; Subway wrappers; old, wrinkled receipts; etc. I obviously had a bad feeling about the pizza inside, hygiene-wise. The location was hidden, and some Italians were outside smoking: I had a really bad impression. But as soon I got out of the car and walked in the door of Carmine's Pizzeria, I smelled pizza. The smell was so intense I could almost taste the pizza. That's how awesome the aroma was.

When I looked around the room, I saw a couple of benches with tables near the door and the windows. The cashier was in the center of the room, and the kitchen was right behind the cashier. To the right of the cashier, who was sitting at a long table, were all the types of pizza they sold. I was shocked at the size of the pizzas. They were huge, nothing like the pizzas Domino's sells. While I was looking at the pizza, we headed to the counter, but there were people in front of us. The people in front showed me how the process went. First, you chose the topping, and then the chef got the slice and put it in the big oven behind the cashier. Then the cashier gave you a tray and a paper plate with your pizza.

After the customers in front of us were done, it was my turn. I asked which tasted the best, and my aunt said the chicken did. So I ended up ordering the chicken. After I ordered, the chef went through the whole process all over again with my cousin and my aunt. When my aunt paid, I thought, *Wow, even the price is cheap*. After that, the three of us went to look for a place to sit down. It was easy to find benches and tables since there weren't a lot of people in the restaurant. My slice smelled so good that I sat down and just stared at it. But the texture was so exotic, like nothing I had ever seen before.

The texture was odd, man! The pizza sauce was striped—the cheese sauce was white and the tomato sauce was red. The taste was amazing, the best part of the pizza. The huge slice was crunchy, hot, and spicy. The crust was crunchy, yet soft. When I chewed, there was a juicy-dry taste; the crunchy crust with the white sauce was good. This was the best pizza I had ever tasted. I never thought my experience at Carmine's Pizzeria was going have an impact on the way I ate, but it did. This experience was the most memorable eating experience I've ever had because I was out of my home state tasting the best pizza I'd ever tasted.

It Has to Be Perfect

Engelle Valenzuela

When I think of gumbo, I think of the sweet and salty sea smell coming fresh off the stove top, filling the air like ambrosia. I remember how my family members and I shove our way through the kitchen to get that very first bowl, and how nothing stops us from going back for seconds, if there is any left. What saddens me, though, is that this day does not happen very often.

Gumbo originated in South Louisiana. It is a stew or soup, poured over rice, that consists primarily of seafood or chicken with different vegetables. Although gumbo looks like a simple dish, it is very time-consuming and takes a lot of patience to make. There are many ingredients that go into creating this very delectable dish. Many people like to put their own little twist on how they make gumbo, so the ingredients can vary.

On the corner of Crenshaw and Rodeo is a Ralphs where my mom and I go to get the ingredients for my grandmother when it's time for her to make a fresh pot of her delicious, tantalizing gumbo. When choosing which ingredients go into the gumbo, we have to think about how we want it to taste: Do we want it very spicy or mostly mild? Do we want more of a seafoodlike or a meaty taste? Does the brand name matter or not?

The ingredients my grandmother normally uses to make her gumbo are chicken, crab legs, celery, sausage, okra, roux (oil and flour), chicken broth, shrimp, rice, and different spices. When my mother and I enter Ralphs, I instantly feel the coolness and smell the fishy smell that fills the whole store. When we walk over to the produce section, my mom takes little, short baby steps, passing each type of chicken along the way. She stops at the packaged chicken breast and closely examines each one she picks up. "Why do you take so long to choose a chicken?" I ask as she stops at the side of the aisle with the cart in front of her, gazing longingly at one particular chicken breast.

"You have to choose everything carefully. I look to see if the chicken is a pinkish color. If it looks like it has been frozen too long, then it is probably not good," she replies. "Also, choose very wisely when it comes to price and how many come in a pack…" While she is explaining this to me, she holds up two packaged chicken breasts, pointing out the differences and telling me why one is a better pick than the other.

Not only does my mom take a long time to choose chicken, she takes a long time to choose *everything*. Sometimes I can be a bit impatient, but I have to look at the bigger picture: the gumbo. It has to be perfect. When choosing crab legs, we look for price, size, and how fresh the crab looks. When we look for sausages, we look at the price and the color. Are they a reddish color, or do they look faded? For celery, we look to see how fresh it is because we chop it up into little pieces to put inside the gumbo. For okra, we choose the ones in the frozen packages. We get canned chicken broth and look for a can that's the right size. For the rice, we choose white rice that comes in a package. Roux plays an important part because it gives the texture of the soup part of the gumbo. It makes it a little thick, more like a stew. My grandma makes the roux from scratch, using flour and oil.

Going grocery shopping for gumbo is a long and hard process. I do not like it, but somebody has to do it, and since I want to eat it, that somebody might as well be me—and my mom.

Our Tradition

Priscilla Lira

My family loves making big meals for occasions like Thanksgiving or Christmas or New Year's. We're a big family, and we like having leftovers. If my mom is going to cook, then she makes a list of groceries that she wants me and my older sister to buy at the Ralphs that's near our house. We take my sister's car even though it's only a block away. We could walk, but since we get a lot of groceries, they get kind of heavy.

It's fun to gather food; looking for groceries is like a scavenger hunt. When we're getting the groceries, we like to explore the whole store and buy goodies for ourselves—doughnuts, Starbucks coffee, frozen pizza, and yogurt—but we don't eat them all in one day. We start preparing the food once we bring my mom's groceries home.

One of the reasons I love Thanksgiving, Christmas, and New Year's is that there's a lot of food to choose from. On Thanksgiving, everyone in my family takes something to my aunt's house. I take pumpkin pie from Coco's, and my mom takes beverages, potato salad, and macaroni salad. My aunt makes turkey and ham. She adds a special sauce that looks like gravy; she calls it "the Juice." The ham she cooks is really delicious: it's sweet, and the slices are very soft. After we consume the meal, there is still dessert: we have apple and pumpkin pie with vanilla ice cream or whipped cream. All of us share. That's our tradition—gathering and sharing food.

There are many foods we have on a regular basis, and spaghetti is one of them. My family and I have it every other week, so it is not something we eat too often. Usually, there is something for dinner that one person doesn't like, but spaghetti is something my whole family can agree on.

When school is almost out, I am very hungry and thinking of what I want to eat when I go home. At this time my mother is at Ralphs with my youngest sister Vanessa, getting what she needs to make spaghetti. She grabs the oil, the tomato sauce (because we prefer that over spaghetti sauce), the salt, the butter, and of course, the spaghetti. We also need something to drink when eating, so she gets some soda or juice, like Thirst Rockers or Pepsi.

When I walk home with my sister Jazmyne, we see our mom and Vanessa at the car calling us to get the grocery bags. Later, inside the house, I pass the time waiting for the spaghetti by first doing homework and then playing video games, drawing, and watching TV. I try to look for something to eat because I am so hungry, but I have to wait until dinner is ready. While I pass the time, my older brother Xavier leaves to go out with his friends, as always, so he'll miss out on eating dinner while it is fresh.

My mother likes cooking dinner most of the time, and she is very generous with us. She gets some rest before cooking because she has to get ready for work, too. She normally does this on a weekday before going to work, even though she would rather stay home to spend time with us. When my mom is ready to cook, she puts the ingredients out on the counter and a pot on the stove, filled up halfway with water. After that, she puts salt and oil into the pot so the spaghetti will have that salty flavor without having to add salt afterward. When the water starts to boil, she breaks the spaghetti in half and puts it in the pot. When the strands are soft, she pours them into a strainer to let the water out. She puts them back into the pot and adds a stick of butter for better flavor. When my mom calls me, I go to help her add the tomato sauce.

When my mom and I finish, Jazmyne, Vanessa, and I stand 'round the pot of spaghetti with our bowls, our mouths watering and stomachs growling. We occasionally have something on the side to eat like chicken, but spaghetti alone is good. I like to drink something while I eat, so I go to the fridge to get some cold, sweet green lime punch. The spaghetti is warm and salty with no extra ingredients to ruin the delicious flavor. It's just me, Jazmyne, and Vanessa eating and watching an everyday weekday program like *The Simpsons* or *Family Guy*.

It is a delightful dinner, very enjoyable, and I enjoy every bite of spaghetti and every sip of punch. Later, Xavier comes home to have some spaghetti, and I come back once again to the kitchen to finish it off. The dinner is so simple, yet it tastes so delicious. If I could enjoy all food like my mom's spaghetti, every day would be a good day.

1. FIRST YOU PUT TOMATO SAUCE.
2. THEN YOU PUT THE CHEESE.
3. NEXT ARE PEPPERONI & MEAT.
4. YOU HAVE TO ADD THE VEGGIES.

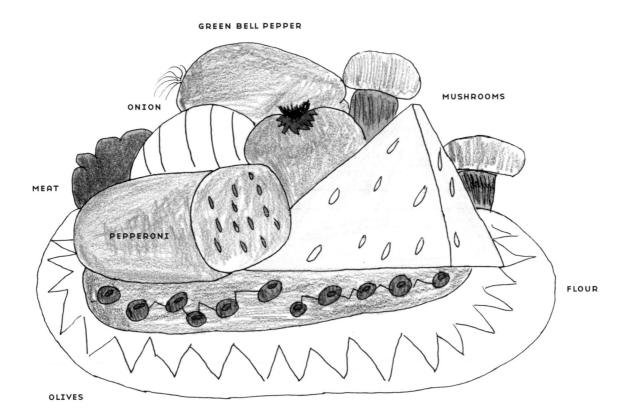

5. THEN YOU COOK IT.
6. NOW YOU HAVE PIZZA.

BRIAN YOUNG

A violent shake wakes me. I reluctantly open my eye to find my little brother Byran in front of me. "Mama called," he says, as I grab the covers and fling them back over myself. "Mama said we gotta come downstairs and get the groceries." I look at the clock; it's 11:30 p.m. I had only been asleep for about forty-five minutes. It doesn't feel like anything more than a few seconds have passed. In a bit of a grumpy mood I get up, put on my jeans, and slide on my Chucks. It's the first week of December. With the celebrations that come with December and the special meals that come with those celebrations, the number of groceries we will have to bring up will be double the usual…maybe triple. Brandon, Angela, Byran, and I step out the door and head toward the elevator (being careful not to make too much noise as we exit because we do not want to wake Brandy, who is terrified of being in the house by herself). Being inside a warm house has made me forget it is winter. The night is especially cold. I don't want to turn around and go get a coat; we are too close to the elevator. I push the call button. Lucky for us, the elevator is already on our floor, so we don't have to wait.

My mother works at the Superior Grocers on 88th and Western as a cashier. Not a pristine job, but it keeps the bills paid and us well fed, so I never complain. She sometimes goes shopping after her shift is finished. That night she happened to have the late shift. I knew ahead of time she was going shopping that night, but I allowed myself to fall asleep anyway.

Once we reach the ground floor, we head straight to the garage. My mother is just pulling in. She stops the silver station wagon in front of us with her music still blasting. Even though the windows on the station wagon are tinted, we can easily see the car is filled with yellow plastic bags with *Superior* stamped on them. Without a word, she pops open the trunk and unlocks the back doors. Without a word, we begin unloading the car. This has become a habitual event. Brandon takes out the two jugs of milk and uses them to prop open the elevator door. We start getting everything out of the back seats first. Being careful not to smash the Sara Lee bread or drop the eggs, I place them in front of the elevator. Then Byran brings the bags with cereal. Angela grabs the Charmin Ultra Soft toilet paper and Bounty paper towels; Brandon, being the candy fiend he is, grabs the stuffed bag full of my mom's Snickers, my Goobers, Byran's Reese's, his Kit-Kats, Angela's M&M's, Brandy's Sour Punches, and various other sweets. He can't wait to satisfy his aching sweet tooth. We continue taking everything out of the back seat until it is empty. Next, it is time to take on the trunk and the treasures it holds. The trunk is where the heavy items are: cases of Coca-Cola, Sprite, Dr. Pepper, and A&W root beer (my personal soda of choice), seven cases of Niagara drinking water, and a few gallons of Minute Maid juice are waiting to be unloaded. One by one we place them alongside the other groceries. Then my mother parks the car in her parking space on the opposite side of the garage. We load up the elevator and head back up to the second floor.

When we reach our destination, we rapidly empty the elevator. Everyone grabs as many of the plastic bags as they can, turning our arms into yellow sleeves. Loading up helps reduce the number of times we have to walk between the house and the elevator. Once all of the bags make it to the house, Byran, Brandon, and I carry in the multiple cases of soda and water. Then we begin playing a complicated game of Tetris trying to fit everything in its place. Cocoa Puffs, Cheerios, Frosted Flakes, Trix, Apple Jacks, and Froot Loops go on top of the fridge. Hormel chili, Chicken of the Sea tuna, Chef Boyardee ravioli, Campbell's chicken noodle soup, and Cup O' Noodles fill the cabinets to the point where there is no space between shelves. The fridge is filled with lettuce, tomatoes, watermelon, apples, Toaster Strudel, milk, buttermilk, eggs, and so many other items that we have to force the door closed.

Afterward I march right into my room and dive into my bed. It's 12:10 now, and I can't go back to sleep.

THE I-DON'T-KNOW BOWL

Mystery and adventure—pray the end product is edible.

Ice Cream Surprise!

Rika R. Thibodeaux

When I am really in the mood for something sweet and delicious, I always make my Ice Cream Surprise—at least that's what I call it. My mom says it's just diabetes in a bowl. This delicious and non-nutritious dessert consists of whatever I have in the house that's sweet. Usually we always have the same things in the kitchen, so my Ice Cream Surprise has the same ingredients. Only once in a while do I get to substitute one thing for something else.

To start, I get the salad bowl out of the top cabinet on the left-hand side of the kitchen along with a really big spoon. I gather my ice cream—chocolate, vanilla, and strawberry; yum!—my Cap'n Crunch cereal, maple syrup, whipped cream, and M&M's. First goes the main part of the entire dessert—the ice cream. After that, the Cap'n Crunch cereal is crunched up and added to the bowl. I then add the M&M's and whipped cream, and top it all off with the maple syrup (preferably Mrs. Butterworth's).

And there it is! The most spectacular, delicious, and non-nutritious meal I have ever encountered in my life!

Wasabi Blues

Jamise Caesar

Wasabi. I hate wasabi. I quiver at the sight of it. Its maliciously potent aroma makes me anxious, and its faded, tinge-of-vomit green hue makes me nauseous. I haven't suffered very many traumas in my life, but the moment I had the misfortune of enduring the "unique taste" of wasabi is definitely among the few of my physically and mentally scarring ordeals.

It began on a fateful day in July, around four o'clock. We were deathly hungry, and the cupboards were barer than an infant born to nudist parents. My uncle suggested we go to an amazing sushi joint: Ziki's was the name. Of course, my aunt and I complied out of sheer starvation. So began the journey I would soon rue.

At first glance the establishment seemed to be an amazing place to dine, but that misconception was quickly dispelled. We ordered hibachi steak, shrimp, and tuna prepared in an array of ways. Indeed, the food was fantastic as my uncle had promised. The texture of the cold, raw fish was not as chewy and over-bearing as I had suspected, and strangely, the Benihana style in which the adeptly poised chef seared the steak and shrimp didn't bother me. The dangerously extreme heat emanating from the skillet/table certainly surpassed all safe-for-physical-contact levels, yet I had every faith in the cook not to char my skin beyond recognition. (In retrospect, I regret enjoying his fabulous cooking so much because I've just won the battle with my parents regarding my desire to become a vegetarian.) Anyway, the threatening sizzle of the scorching grill only excited me. After the chef—with ah acrobatic flick of his wrist—tossed a shrimp into my aunt's mouth, he took a break to let us enjoy our meal as a family. I wish this had been the end of my Ziki's dining experience. I would have appreciated and cherished that. Sadly, it was only a misleading prelude to the terror to come.

My uncle sat back, patted his full stomach with a grunt of gratitude, and picked the tidbits of steak from his teeth. My aunt gleamed with satisfaction, and I was stuffed beyond a fourteen-year-old's intestinal capacity. We were done. The waiter brought our check, and we began to leave.

Suddenly, my uncle realized that the fancy saucer of thinly sliced spicy ginger and a looming clump of, yes, *wasabi* were still resting menacingly on the table. In jolly seriousness, my uncle dared me to inhale the entire cluster while keeping a straight face for twenty whole dollars (as a fourteen-year-old, twenty dollars meant a wide-eyed *chi-ching!*).

At that exact moment, there must have been an eerie draft. There simply was not enough thinking time between the dare and the execution. Before I could express doubt, I shoved the mountain of greenish goop into my mouth.

To say the least, my tongue was burnt to oblivion; it sizzled until my taste buds lost the will to live, grew numb, and died. It was total and utter mouth burn, worse than early-morning, shock-inducing, scalding coffee. It felt unnatural, like I was about to pass away shortly after. Sadly, I did fear for my health during my noticeable lapse of judgment both before and during the wasabi fiasco.

Today you couldn't pay me a million dollars to consume that rancid death trap disguised as food. Alas, 'til this day, I still ask myself, *Why?!* If I had known then what I know now, I would have never taken my uncle up on that bet.

I guess I really needed the money.

WHEN WE'RE CRAVING PIZZA

IVANNA RODRIGUEZ

My favorite food is pizza from Grandma Lucia's in Culver City. It is the only place my family and I go to when we're craving pizza. One day, when we were driving through Culver City, we came across this little Italian restaurant and decided to go in and check it out. None of us had ever been there or seen it before. We walked into the restaurant, and the first thing we saw were these large glass windows that allowed us to look inside the kitchen. We could see how they were preparing the food, so we thought that was interesting. We had never been to a pizza place like that, so we were intrigued.

When we walked in, they were rolling out the freshly made dough, not frozen dough like they use in most other pizza places. When we smelled the pizza, our mouths automatically started to water. When we looked at the menu, we saw all different kinds of fresh ingredients you can put on your pizza, like mushrooms, onions, bell peppers, pineapple, italian sausage, and sun-dried tomatoes. Besides pizza they also had all sorts of pastas, sandwiches, and other Italian foods on the menu. We ordered two large pizzas. One of them had pepperoni, mushrooms, and bell peppers on it; the other one had pineapple and chicken on it. They used 100 percent real mozzarella cheese and generous toppings. When we took our first bite of the pizza, we immediately tasted all of the fresh ingredients.

The pizza tasted like no other pizza we had ever tasted before. It was much different from what we would get at any other pizza place, like Pizza Hut or Domino's. The crust was crunchy, but not hard or burned. The slices were big and packed with ingredients, and everyone seemed to be enjoying it. Even my little sister liked it, and she's a really picky eater. Ever since that day, Grandma Lucia's is the only place we get our pizza from.

The location is small and kind of hidden, so you don't really expect the food to be that good. They have a couple of tables inside, so you can eat there if you want, but they also provide free delivery. I believe that the best way to eat it is to take it home and put your favorite hot sauce on top of all the other ingredients, even though it still tastes great with nothing else on it. If you have never put hot sauce on your pizza, then you should because it tastes very good.

STUFFED

STEPHANIE OVERTON

The first time I made stuffed shells, my cousin and I went shopping together at Ralphs, and we had a wonderful time in the store. My cousin is smart, funny, and just a great person. We were joking around and just having fun. It's fun shopping because it's great to spend time with the people you love.

I couldn't wait until we got home because I wanted to hurry up and make and eat this dish. On the car ride home, I also thought about how when I got back to California, I would go shopping every month so I could make stuffed shells.

Now, whenever I go to the supermarket, I shop at Ralphs because it's big and there are lots of foods to choose from. The first thing I get for the stuffed shells is two bags of spinach—that's the best part. I am not a big fan of spinach, but the first time I ate stuffed shells with it, it was so amazing. When you bite into the shells, the soft spinach is so wonderful that you never want the taste to end. The next thing that I get is two boxes of shells. It doesn't matter what kind of shells you get just as long as they're the large kind. Then I get two packs of ground turkey, one carton of eggs, one container of ricotta cheese, one pack of Mexican cheese, and one jar of spaghetti sauce (I usually get Prego). Finally, I get parsley. Getting the ingredients for this dish is very easy, and the taste is always to die for.

After coming back from Ralphs, my cousin and I organized all of our ingredients. If you are not organized, you will mess up the whole meal. First, my cousin preheated the oven to 350 degrees. Then she brought a pot of water (about six cups) to boil. After the water was boiling, she added one teaspoon of salt and about twenty-five large shells. My cousin always boils her pasta shells until they are tender but not all the way done. When finished, the shells are the size of an egg.

Then she started cooking the ground turkey. My cousin placed the two packs of ground turkey into a one-inch-deep skillet for fifteen to twenty minutes, until golden brown. The smell of the ground turkey was so delightful with all of the different kinds of seasonings. When my cousin made the ground turkey, she added several types of spices: garlic salt, seasoned salt, and lemon pepper.

While my cousin was making the ground turkey, I wanted to eat the whole thing. When the pasta was done, we drained the shells and set them under cold water until we were ready to use them. The best part of the whole thing was combining the ground turkey, ricotta cheese, Mexican cheese, spinach, tomato sauce, and two eggs. After everything was combined, I put in about one teaspoon of salt. I couldn't wait until the stuffed shells were done because I was really hungry and it felt like I hadn't eaten all day.

Then we started stuffing the shells. We took a small spoon and used it to put the mixture inside the cooked shells. We put tons of cheese and about a half cup of tomato sauce on top of the stuffed shells, and then we put it in the oven for about thirty minutes.

***

I enjoyed this dish so much that I still remember it, and I had it three years ago. That's how great this meal was. Preparing it was fun because I never got to spend time with my cousin. Making this meal with her was the most amazing time I ever had. While preparing this meal, my cousin and I couldn't stop laughing. I hope that we can do this again.

THIS MEAL CALLED PHO

GARY PAUL BURBRIDGE III

Pho (Vietnamese noodle soup) is a delicious meal that I had for the first time a very long time ago. It was right after a special baseball game, the semifinals in Little League. Unfortunately, I lost the game. I was heartbroken and felt really bad losing in front of my mother, who had been cheering me on, screaming so loud. I cried myself to sleep in the back of the car on our way home, waking up with the taste of salty teardrops in my mouth.

Surprisingly, my mom hadn't taken us home. Instead she had driven us to a weird-looking restaurant that was very warm inside with a positive vibe. This restaurant was different, with all kinds of statues, masks on the walls, and other decorations. I almost forgot how terrible a game I had just played. The food was similar to the food I was raised on, noodles because of hard times, so it was natural.

Pho is a meal that you can customize to suit yourself. When you order you'll get a bowl of hot broth, but the rest of your food comes in a take-home container. Thin-sliced beef, shrimp, rice noodles, bean sprouts, and cilantro are the basics that come with the meal package. Of course, you can have additional things at a higher price, but these are the basic pho requirements. Just add your own spices to make it taste best for you. You can also add all kinds of healthy vegetables to make it taste as fresh as it looks.

The pho consists of thin, pale, almost-clear, slimy noodles. Have a napkin prepared for the juices gushing everywhere as you devour this meal in great haste because of its taste. In addition to the juicy noodles, there is orange and spicy-but-sweet shrimp. But you're not even close to done yet, there is also semi-cooked beef. Did I mention that the shrimp is semi-cooked as well? Nothing in this meal is fully cooked until you finish it off by putting it in the blazing container of broth it comes with.

The taste will make your heart sing, and once your eye gets a glimpse of it, your stomach will scream, anxiously waiting for you to eat it. Your taste buds will yearn for the first bite, and your nose will love the aroma. It clears up your chest and can also clear up your nose if you have a vicious cold that needs to be taken care of. Holding the bowl of food in your hands, it is hot as hell, but it's worth it. It's a little piece of heaven.

If you love it like I do, you can make it yourself. The broth is a very important component of the meal. It's made from simmering beef or chicken; choose what fits your taste. I'm more of a beef guy. I just love the flavor; it's like doing my taste buds a favor. You set the bones from chicken, beef, or some type of meat into water to mix and marinate. This gives some flavor. Cut up some onions for the mix, as you would usually do when making soup, to give it that kicking spice and flavor. There are a lot more seasonings that you can use for the broth, but I only use the basics since that's what I'm used to and love.

When you order it, the steak comes very thinly sliced so that it can cook well in the bowl of hot steaming broth. The secret of cutting the meat is to cut across the grain. You want your meat slices as thin as possible. You can always throw the whole chunk of meat in the freezer for a little while so that it's easier to slice thinly. Don't forget about the shrimp; they are a delight, even though there are only a few, about five to seven.

I'm going to stop right here with all the details. My stomach is growling and my mouth is watering. I'm a lot older than when I first tried this meal; a lot of things have changed. I don't play baseball anymore. After that losing game I basically quit playing, right along with crying over events like that. But one thing I never quit is buying, eating, and loving this meal called pho.

THE GREAT TASTE OF CEVICHE

OLGA DeLeTORRE

It was six on a foggy Saturday morning. My annoying younger brothers had a soccer game. They were packing cleats into their gym bags and changing into their soccer uniforms. Finally, they finished dressing, so they got out of the house and into my mom's 2004 Yukon XL. On the way to the game, my mom saw a painted sign for Mexican tacos, fish, and coctel (shrimp cocktail). She started thinking of ceviche. Then she said, "Oyen niños, ¿quieren hacer camarones en ceviche?" (Hey you guys, do you want to make ceviche?) Everyone said, "Yeah, we'll help you make it." Everyone had a smile on their face. The boys even stopped playing smackdown in the truck. Instead of fighting, they were talking about how they wanted to make ceviche.

We finally got to the soccer field, and the game took about an hour. I wished I could have my favorite food already; I could feel the tasty ceviche in my mouth. My brothers won their soccer game 8–0, so we had a great reason to celebrate! We knew what we had to do, so we got into the truck and went back home. We started looking around the kitchen and making a list of what we needed to make the ceviche. If we missed an ingredient, we knew it wouldn't taste good. We needed to go to the store to get supplies. We needed to get tomatoes, onions, cucumbers, cilantro, avocado, lemons, and camarones (shrimp). When my dad came home, I told him that my little brothers won the soccer game, so we were going to make ceviche. He asked what he could do to help, so I gave him the list and asked him to go to the market. We knew that we had picked the right person to get the ingredients because Tecomán, Colima, Mexico, where my dad is from, is all about the seafood. Since he was a kid, he helped my grandma make it. This is a family tradition from my dad's family. His mom made it with her mom, my dad made it with his mom, and now our family is making it with my dad.

My dad asked me to go with him to the market to help him get the ingredients. We wanted the ceviche so badly that we were all helping. We live around 3rd Avenue, and the store is on 6th Avenue, so we took Jefferson and 4th to get there faster and not get stuck in traffic. We got there in about four minutes. The store is not big like Food 4 Less, Albertsons, or Vons. It's a little store that my friend owns with her family called Lupita's Market. I like buying everything right there because they have everything we need to make our ceviche. When I was getting the ingredients I needed, I saw a lot of different things. I saw people walking in the store, trying to fit into a door that only one person can fit through at a time. I saw a man who worked there take orders from people, but he forgot whose turn it was, so people started to argue. This place has everything in order; there is a small place for their fruit, milk, meat, and everything you might need. The store smells okay, but when you get close to the meat, it smells like a weird mixed smell that you can't even describe because of all the different kinds of meat that are there. My sister and I hate the smell of meat that hasn't been cooked. It's still a fresh cut, but when it's cooked, it smells different: it smells good. I got close to the meat, so I held my nose like a five-year-old. The store was loud. You could hear people talking to friends and Mexican music playing. While I was watching everything, I tasted the fresh mint of my gum and saw my dad go around the store. I laughed at him for getting things we never even needed; he's a crazy shopper.

We checked the list twice to make sure we had everything. If we miss one little thing, we can't make the camarones, and nothing will work. Then we checked to see if everything looked good and fresh because if it's not fresh, then why make something that doesn't taste good? Like they say, if you're going to do something, do it right. And don't waste good food. My family doesn't like wasting food. It is sad to see people we don't know who haven't eaten for days, so we don't waste food. Instead, we give it to those people who haven't eaten, people who worked with us before. It's sad seeing them lose their jobs and live on the street. Finally, we paid, got out of the store and into the truck, and my dad drove us home.

We took the bags inside so that we could get started on the ceviche. Everyone did what they knew they needed to do. My mom got the vegetables so she could cut them. I got the camarones to peel so that my sister could cut them into small pieces. My brothers did the lemons. One cut, and the other one squeezed them for juice to cook the camarones in. While we were doing all of that, my dad was trying to clean up the mess for when we would be ready to eat. When my mom was done cutting the vegetables, she came over to help me so I could finish faster. After we were done, we helped my sister cut the camarones. When my brothers finished, we put the camarones in the lemon juice so they could cook fresh and cold. It takes around fifteen to twenty minutes to cook. After that, we put the vegetables together with them. We put them in the freezer so that they could cool faster and we could eat them sooner. It tastes like the first food you have ever tasted before. They taste like something out of this world and make your mouth water. That's what mine had been doing since six in the morning, and it was now around four in the afternoon. It's great to do this for three reasons: we worked as a family to make it, we all helped each other, and we were all going to eat it together.

As we all ate together, we felt close. No one was fighting, and everyone was happy, watching TV and making jokes. Even my uncle came to eat after work. We all ate as a big family. It was loud with every kind of music: hip-hop, rock, and even Spanish music. My family might be made of different people, but we are close when it comes to working together. We make this dish because all of our family is here to help, with big smiles on our faces, and we work together to do something everyone loves.

YUCA CON CHICHARRÓN

INGREDIENTS:

SALT & PEPPER FOR TASTE
OIL FOR FRYING PORK
3 TORTILLAS PER PERSON

CHICHARRÓN (PORK RIND)
CHOPPED INTO 3" STRIPS

SALAD:
TOMATO 1/4" SLICE
CABBAGE 1" LONG & THIN
ONION 1/4" CUBE
LETTUCE 1" LONG & THIN
SQUISH OF LEMON

YUCA (CASSAVA) 4" LONG
BOIL UNTIL SOFT

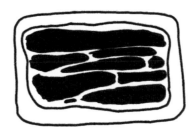

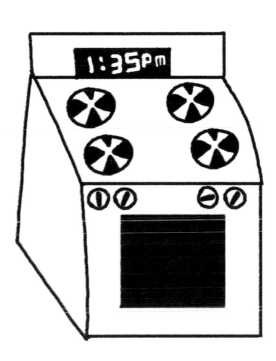

Morning Breakfast

Marresha Milner

Sometimes my mother and I make a big breakfast for the whole family: pancakes, scrambled eggs, biscuits, potatoes with cheese and green onions, turkey sausage, bacon, and so much more. We usually cook on a weekend when we are feeling great. Mom and I wake up at six in the morning to go to the store. To many that may seem early, but we are used to it. I really enjoy going to the store and cooking with my mom; we've always done these things together. In my mind it's sort of a tradition that brings back so many memories from when I was a little girl, not only when we're in the kitchen but also when we're in the store. In the kitchen, I would watch her cook, and I would say to myself, *I sure wish I could do everything she does.* And in the store, I could never reach the things on the high shelves. Now that I've grown big enough to reach them, I say to myself, *Finally!*

Before we head to the store, we go into the kitchen and see what we already have. We realize that we have many of the things we need: eggs, cheese, milk, black pepper, and garlic salt. After we see what we have, we make a list of what we need. We put on our shoes and jackets, get in the car, and drive to the store, playing music as we ride. We always go to Ralphs on Rodeo and La Brea, and we always try to get a close parking space.

Once we park and step inside, I grab either a handbasket or a cart, depending on how many things we need. As soon as we walk in the door, I smell the bread and cakes and cookies. I try my hardest to ignore the wonderful smells and head straight to the baking aisle to get a box of Bisquick pancake mix. It's our favorite. Then we go over to the produce section to get scallions (or as we call them, green onions). Next, we head over to the other side of the store in search of the meat. Once we reach the meat section, we pick up turkey sausages and the small red and white package of Farmer John bacon. We never get beef because we feel it's unhealthy, and we just don't eat it. After we find the meat, we go and look for the Red Yukon potatoes, which are always funny looking. They look dirty and lumpy, but they taste delicious. I always get that specific brand because it's my favorite. After we've found the potatoes, we pick up a jar of Welch's grape jelly and either a quart or gallon of Minute Maid orange juice.

Now we head over to the checkout lines. Usually the lines are long, and it takes what seems like forever to get to the cashier. I become so anxious while in line, standing there thinking about eating the delicious food when I get home. I get super happy when I watch the cashier scan every item and the bagger bag the groceries. My mom finally pays for everything, and we carry out the bags to the car, open the trunk, put them in, and get in the car. We turn on the radio and head on home with our minds focused on cooking and eating a delicious breakfast.

JAIBA: ONE-OF-A-KIND CRAB SALAD

BLANCA REYES

On a hot day I was hanging out with my neighbor Liseth. Her mom prepared a dish I had never heard of before in my life, jaiba! She offered me some just so I could taste it and see if I liked it. I took a bite, and my head started spinning with so many different yummy flavors. It was crunchy, soft, sour, juicy, and spicy all at the same time. At that moment jaiba became my favorite food of all. After that bite I couldn't resist and ended up with like five tostadas filled with jaiba on my plate. I devoured them.

Before I left, I asked Liseth's mom for the recipe so I could prepare jaiba for my family. Can't you just picture a fresh-tasting crab salad mixed with many vegetables? It goes great with any kind of drink you prefer.

When I prepare the salad, I shop for the ingredients at Ranch Market. The market has everything I need; I can even buy a package of crab that is already out of the shell. I always buy a foil pan to mix the ingredients together in, but you can use any pan you want, depending on how much you're planning to make.

The very first thing you do is break down the crab into small pieces. Soak the crab in lemon so it can cook in the juice for about fifteen minutes, until it can't absorb any more. You will see a little bit of the lemon juice left on the sides. While that's happening you can start cutting up the onions, tomatoes, cilantro, cucumber, and celery into small pieces. Small squares would be perfect, but don't cut them too tiny because that will take away the juice from the vegetables. You want to retain the juice so you can taste the vegetables in the salad. You also want to be able to see the vegetables: they give the salad color and make it look pretty. Like they say, "People eat with their eyes."

Add the salt, black pepper, and Clamato after putting the vegetables in the salad. (When buying the Clamato, make sure to buy the one with the jalapeño flavor. If you don't, then your salad might just taste like a lot of tomato sauce.) For those who like spicy foods, you can also slice up some jalapeños—the little kind—and toss them in. Last, peel the shells off the shrimp, boil them in water, let them cool off, and then mix them with the salad. I love shrimp. In my opinion the shrimp are what make the salad taste so delicious. But don't get me wrong; if you're not a fan, without them the salad still tastes pretty yummy.

Finally, you're done! All your hard work will pay off; trust me. You can eat the jaiba with a tostada and put Tapatio on top—it tastes so delicious that you might as well prepare yourself five tostadas to start off. You can also make the dish even tastier by adding some guacamole. Prepare yourself a drink, and sitting in front of you is a one-of-a-kind crab salad tostada. Enjoy!

THE BRC
(BEANS, RICE, AND CHEESE) BURRITO

Not incredibly healthy, but intensely gratifying.

Burgers for Breakfast

KENDRA GLOVER

This is not a story about gumbo. Nor is it a story about tamales. This is about plain ol' hamburgers. For as long as I can remember, I've loved hamburgers. McDonald's and Jack in the Box were like my second home. However, no hamburger compares to my parents' home-cooked, ground-beef hamburgers.

One day, like any other day, I awoke to the monstrous cries of my stomach.

"What do you want for breakfast?" my dad asked, as if he didn't already know.

"Hamburgers!" I exclaimed.

"Of course you do," my dad laughed.

I opened the fridge hoping to retrieve the ground beef, but to my dismay, there was none. Here I was with nothing to fill my insatiable hunger. Sure, there was cereal, as well as oatmeal, but who eats that for breakfast? Not me. I wanted my hamburger.

"Daddy, please can we go to the store to buy some more ground beef?" I whined.

"Sure, right after I take my shower."

Oh gosh. Not a shower. My dad always took too long.
After about thirty minutes of waiting, my dad and I set out on bikes to R-Ranch Market. He would occasionally send worrisome glances when I rode past him. When we got to R-Ranch, we bought more than we had come for and rode home with our bike handles full of groceries.
After putting away all the food, my dad began taking out the ingredients.

"Daddy, I'm already ten," I said. "I'm old enough to cook without you or Mom. Can I make one myself?"

"Sure, but make sure you watch it," he said as he walked away.

It was my first time making hamburgers, but having watched my mom and dad cook them countless times, I knew what to do. Or at least I thought I did.

I put the patty in the skillet and walked away from the stove. After waiting a while for it to cook, I decided it was time to flip it. I walked up to the stove and noticed my hamburger was on fire. I quickly ran out the kitchen screaming, "Fireeee!"

My uncle, who had been sitting on the couch, got up and yelled for me to put it out, but all I could do was cower in fear. My dad then rushed over and put the fire out by putting the skillet in water.

After that experience, I never cooked another hamburger again—at least not without the help of my mom or dad.

GERMAN CHOCOLATE HEAVEN

JALISA "JUJU" MILLER

Usually when my mom and I decide to make german chocolate cake, it can only mean one thing: a special occasion. We rarely get to have this cake, so when we do, it's so satisfying. Before we start baking, I check and see which ingredients we need. We always have the pecans, vanilla flavor, and eggs. We almost never have the cake mix, though. Now, when it comes to cake, we are all about the brand in my house—Betty Crocker, to be exact. Nobody does it like Betty Crocker: her cake mixes always come out wonderful, never any lumps or bumps, and they're so delicious. We also use evaporated milk and Almond Joy coconut. This brand of coconut makes the icing taste just right because of the moistness of the coconut, my mom says.

So, once I've figured out what we need to buy, it's time

to go to the grocery store. We go to the Superior Market on Florence and Compton. We don't go to any other market over there because Superior Market has the best deals ever. It takes us about seven minutes to get there; it's a pretty smooth ride as we pass through two major lights, Slauson and Gage. "Jeesa, make a list of the stuff we need for the cake, and look at that big chicken!" my mom says as we pass Pollo Campero, a chicken place. We pass another grocery store and a recycling center. We don't go to the other grocery store because it's always so crowded and the checkout lines are down the aisles.

The parking lot at Superior Market is always a madhouse. We usually drive around once or twice before finding a parking space. Or my mom sends me into the store while she waits for one. When you walk in, smells of sweet pastries and fresh tortillas fill your nose. I rush over to grab a fresh tortilla, which smells of corn and flour. The scent may be great, but it tastes even better, especially when you put a little bit of sour cream on it. After the tortillas, I slowly creep toward the pastries. Decorative cakes and parfaits fill my eyes; they look so pretty. Cookies and breads dance before me on silver platters. After looking at all the pastries, I stop at the produce section.

After having all this fun, I wander to the cake aisle; all I have in my mind now is the red Betty Crocker box. I have cleared my mind of everything but that cake-mix box. The only things that can distract me are the bags of coconut, which I love to poke. After I get the cake mix, my mom and I head on home.

Don't Let the Fruit Fool You

Alysa R. Drew

There's nothing like the sweet smell of peach cobbler on Thanksgiving Day. You know it from the moment you wake up and smell the sugary, sweet peaches on the stove along with the buttery, soft dough in the oven.

The enjoyment I get out of helping my mom make this amazing mouth-watering dessert is almost as good as eating it. The day before Thanksgiving, we go to Smart & Final to pick up sugar to make the peaches nice and sweet. We also buy Krusteaz pie crust to put the peaches in so that you can have the sweet flavor of the peaches and the buttery crust at the same time. We buy vanilla extract and a lemon to squeeze into the peaches to give the cobbler a nice tangy-and-sweet taste. We also buy butter and cinnamon to give the crust and peaches an old-school, mouth-watering taste. Then we add the nutmeg to the peaches—another sweet taste! We can't forget the aluminum pans that we cook the delicious dessert in. After we buy all of the ingredients, we buy Breyers vanilla bean ice cream to top off the hot, sweet, buttery peach cobbler.

Don't let the fruit fool you—this dish is as healthy as a bag of candy.

MY OWN FRESH, TASTY WAY

ISAIRA PADILLA

My favorite food is seafood. Specifically, cocktail shrimp became my favorite after my Aunt Silvia served it at a family reunion in San Francisco about two months ago. It was so good that when I had my first bite of shrimp and the shrimp juice, I instantly tasted the cilantro, lemon juice, and just the right amount of hot sauce.

Since my visit to San Francisco, I decided to make my own cocktail shrimp. I'm making the shrimp cocktail my own fresh, tasty way: my family loves onions and tomatoes in every dish, but they aren't my favorite, so I leave them out.

I love eating my shrimp cocktail for lunch but not for dinner because it's a really heavy dish. When I'm ready to go shopping for my groceries, I ask my mom to drive me to Smart & Final to buy my ingredients: hot sauce, cilantro, shrimp, lemon, sea salt, and salted crackers. After we buy the ingredients, my mom and I drive back home and unload the truck.

After my mom and I enter the house, I unpack the groceries and wash the cilantro, frozen shrimp, and lemons. Then, I place a pot with water on the stove. Once the water in the pot starts boiling, I add the shrimp and let them cook for twenty-five to thirty minutes. While the shrimp is boiling, I get a chopping board for the cilantro and lemons. Once the shrimp is a pinkish color, it is ready. I take them out of the hot pot and place them into a plastic bowl, letting the shrimp sit for five to ten minutes so they can cool down before I peel them.

While the shrimp is cooling, I start chopping the cilantro into little cubes and cutting the lemons into fourths. Once I'm done cutting them, I put the lemons and cilantro into two small plastic bowls that are to the left side of the cutting board.

When this is all done, I get a very fat and tall glass cup, which I fill halfway with shrimp, a pinch or two of cilantro, and the squirt of an entire lemon. I add a splash of Tapatio—a really hot hot sauce I like much better than other hot sauces—because it's spicier and gives a better taste to my cilantro. I fill the glass cup with some of the juice that the shrimp boiled in and then stir the entire thing together.

Finally, I taste the cocktail shrimp to see if it needs a sprinkle of sea salt. Once it is perfect in every way, I grab the pack of salted crackers because they give a great salty taste to the shrimp cocktail. I just love ending my shrimp cocktail with some salted crackers.

I'm ready to eat.

Camarones a la Diabla

Dana Flores

My favorite food is camarones a la diabla, shrimp with spicy chili and ham. The first time I ate it, I loved it—but when I first looked at it, it looked weird. It looked like it was going to be really spicy, too. It smelled like shrimp and garlic, and it kind of smelled like fish, too. I don't really like fish, so maybe that's why I thought it was going to taste bad. When I touched it, it felt slippery and squishy, but it actually tasted good.

My dad is the one who makes it, but he only makes it when he's in a good mood. I don't really know why, but that's just how he does it. I've never asked him about it before.

My mom and I go to the supermarket together to buy all the ingredients. She always sends me to get the shrimp, but I hate doing that because that section is really cold. I stand in front of the shrimp, just staring at it, thinking about how the spicy shrimp is going to taste. I hurry up and get the shrimp.

I go to my mom and tell her I am ready to go, but she still hasn't looked for the avocado, so I tell her to hurry up. When we're ready to go at the cashier, the little cash-register drawer is stuck and the lady is taking her sweet time. I'm so hungry that all I think about is the food. After five minutes or so they fix the machine, and while my parents are paying, I put all the stuff we bought into the plastic bags they give at the store.

Finally we're in the car, but my dad still has to get gas, so he sends me to tell the lady at the gasoline station that he wants forty dollars in number seven. I run as fast as I can, and now we're in the car again, and I am so happy. When we get home, I unpack all the food.

Then my mom puts the butter in the pan and adds the shrimp. She tells me to start cutting the oranges, onions, cucumbers, lettuce, and lime, and I do it as fast as I can. After fifteen minutes I'm done, and my mom has added a special spicy chili sauce called Valentina to the shrimp.

I go to my room for a while to listen to my iPod, and then my mom walks in and tells me to go to the table because the food is ready. As I am going down the stairs, I hear a lot of people talking, and I think, *There's someone in my house?* I don't really want to go downstairs because I'm a little bit shy, and if I don't know the people who are in my house, I'm going to start blushing.

I finally decide to go, and I see my dad's friend and his son who is my age, so I get even more shy. But I'm hungry, so I keep on going. I say hi to everybody and get my food, but the table is full, so I go to my room to eat.

I sit in my bed with the spoon right in front of my mouth, and I can smell the shrimp and the chili. As I am about to put the spoon in my mouth, I think, *This is probably going to taste nasty,* but I don't mind, so I just keep on going. When I put the food on my tongue, it burns so much, and I scream so loudly that my mom comes into my room. When I tell her what happened, she starts laughing at me. I get mad, but then I pick up the spoon once again and before I put the food in my mouth, I blow on it so it won't be too hot.

Finally, I taste the delicious shrimp and chili. I love it. I'm enjoying every single spoonful that I put in my mouth, and with each bite I get more and more full until I can't eat any more.

JACK WITH MY BFF

JASMINE LITTLEJOHN

Anytime my best friend Taylor and I are walking toward La Brea and Jefferson, we are most likely going to Jack in the Box. My favorite meal, the only one I really enjoy, has a Big Cheeseburger, two tacos, an order of small fries, and a small Coke. I love this meal because I enjoy the time that Taylor and I spend together. We like to end our long and stressful week of school with a treat for ourselves.

Taylor and I visit Jack in the Box on Thursday or Friday night around six. Usually, we gracefully walk to Jack in the Box, but we'll only visit the one on Jefferson because the one on Crenshaw is fifty cents more expensive and does not have that same taste as the other one. It is a special tradition that only Taylor and I have together. Once we are close, I get excited all over again because I can always smell the very fresh tacos from a mile away. We have to cross two lights to get there, so while Taylor is talking to me—about guys, usually—I am mentally focused on the pig-out we will soon share.

Once we arrive at the door, Taylor glances over at me and

asks, "The usual?" I quickly respond, "Yeah." I search for a secluded corner close to the window with a view of our surroundings. This way we see who comes in and who goes out. I love to feel like we are in a bubble, where no one can interrupt our flow. That's the best seat, in my opinion. There are usually older men drinking coffee sitting somewhere in the middle section; it's like that is the sophisticated area. These men are always quiet, using their inside voices. It seems like they're on their lunch break at times.

On school days, teens usually sit outside while businessmen—in their late thirties, it looks like—sit in the middle, giving others their privacy and personal seat selection. Knowing that, it makes it easier for us to have the perfect seat. I sit my bag down to claim that these seats are our thrones until we get up. Taylor sits her bag right across from mine to emphasize that one-on-one, face-to-face time we share together. We enjoy each other's company.

We stay for hours at a time, but to us, it feels like it is never enough. She grabs our cups to fill them up while she stands and waits for our order. I patiently wait as well. When we share a cup, Taylor puts in half lemonade and half Dr. Pepper. She likes juice and I like soda, so she makes a *big* compromise for me. When we get separate cups, Taylor gets lemonade, fruit punch, and Sprite, but she gets plain Coke just for me. When the lady calls our number, I cry out, "Don't forget to ask for extra hot sauce and ranch, Tay," strictly for our burgers and tacos.

Taylor grabs the tray and joins me at the table. She hands me my burger and my tacos, and lastly, dumps both of our small fries onto one tray together, which completes a calm, balanced atmosphere. Sometimes we only get one order of fries to share because we pretend we are trying to watch our figures. Then we say grace: "God is good; God is great. Let us thank him for our food; let it nourish our bodies and strengthen my soul, in Jesus' name, amen." During grace, I tend to pick up a fry or two, hoping she does not notice. I feel like I cannot help myself—that crispy and salty smell dances on the tip of my nose. The temptation forces me to disobey our table rules. After grace, she gives me this stare; once she opens her eyes, she always catches me chewing. I laugh it off every time. By that time, we both put one individual container of ranch dressing and a couple of hot sauce packets on our tacos. I am always the first one to complete this task, so while I am waiting for her to finish, I take a couple of sips of Coca-Cola to kill a couple of seconds in time. I usually pick off some lettuce because it drowns out the natural spices and the taste of the corn shell. I place everything in the order I eat them, so the tacos are always first—my favorite part of the meal.

Taylor and I always take our first bite of the tacos together. The taco is perfect because of its crunchy shell and spicy meat, while the ranch and lettuce give it that cool and fresh taste. Oddly, I love when the hot sauce and ranch drip onto the wrapper of the tacos; I'll always grab two fries and scoop up the mystery sauce I just created. Even though Taylor and I eat at different paces, somehow, we always end up with that last bite at the same point in time.

After the final bite, we'll start up some more conversation while enjoying our fresh-cut french fries and Coke. The fries are always so hot and so moist that I eat them while I am eating the tacos. I'll then drink some cold and refreshing Coca-Cola. Then comes the Big Cheeseburger. We unwrap our burgers neatly, like gifts, and break them right down the center. Taylor pours her ranch sauce directly onto her burger while I simply dip my own like a chip. The burger tastes like it is grilled; it has this overpowering beefy flavor while a subtle tangy taste from the mustard appears. I am usually full by this point, plus the burger is thick, so Taylor knows to be on the lookout for our refills to smoothen things out when eating our meals.

I rarely finish my Big Cheeseburger because I always take a couple of gulps before the last few bites I have left, so I always end up getting full off of soda. By the time I am completely full, Taylor knows, and I look at her with puppy eyes and ask if she wants my last piece because I cannot bear that one last bite. Finally, after we finish eating, we sit for five minutes because our stomachs look like they will explode at any minute if we try to move. After resting, we head home with the satisfaction of our odd, delicious meal. Even though I love the eating experience, the bonding time is what makes it so special. Taylor and I get to spend time together without any distraction from the outside world.

My Home-Style Oven Macaroni

Taylor Broom

Every major family holiday such as Christmas and Thanksgiving, I get to make the delicious home-style macaroni; this is my favorite job. A week in advance, my mom, my two sisters, and I all pile up into the car and make our way to Food 4 Less. This grocery store is the cheapest, and there is no need to spend extra money on food that is only for one day. My mom always gets frustrated and yells at us because there is so much to get done and we are constantly distracting her with our frequent irrelevant questions, like if we can have chips or other goodies that have nothing to do with the list of things we need.

My mom divides the list up between herself, my sisters, and me. My mom gets all the meat for the dinner—she says that we do not know how to choose the good meat and that she does not have time for any screwups. My older sister Kayla gathers all the starches—she already knows exactly what we need without our mom having to tell her. My younger sister Karly gets everything for the desserts. She is the family member with the massive sweet tooth, and she always picks out what she wants. I usually get all the vegetables for the meal because they are the closest to the entrance, and so I do not have to walk all around the store.

Grocery shopping is annoying. There is always someone standing in front of the item that I need, and Patience is not my middle name. We probably spend about two hundred dollars in the two hours that we spend at the store. This experience can be irritating enough to make you want to pull your hair out. Even though it is a hassle, at the end of the day it is both necessary and completely worth it.

When my family gets home, we put away the groceries. A week later, it is time for me to make my holiday specialties: chocolate cake, potato salad, greens, and (of course) home-style oven macaroni. To make my macaroni I need two pounds of Anthony's elbow macaroni, 2 percent reduced-fat milk, two pounds of sharp cheddar cheese, two pounds of monterey jack cheese, one egg, a stick of butter (we use unsalted butter because it does not add any extra flavor), and—last but not least—an entire white onion, with some black pepper to shake on top.

I boil the noodles for about eight to twelve minutes. Once they are ready, I take a strainer and pour the water out of the pot. The noodles are then rinsed off with cold water so they won't continue to cook. I then dump the noodles back into the pot. Some people like to mix all their ingredients together and then add them to the pot, but I mix everything together in the pot. I set the pot on low heat just to melt the ingredients a little, and since I don't know the exact measurements, I eyeball everything—this is how I was taught to cook. When I asked my mom, grandmother, and auntie about the measurements, none of them could tell me a precise amount. As I continue, I add a stick of butter, followed by some milk. I immediately add an egg after the milk; this way the milk will cool down the egg so it won't accidentally scramble. I add the onion that my little sister has chopped up for me and three pounds of cheese. Finally, I mix the noodles with all the ingredients.

The macaroni is dumped into a big thirteen-by-nine-inch pan. The last pound of cheese is added on top, and black pepper is sprinkled over the dish before it's placed into the 400-degree oven. This will cook for about twenty minutes. The pan is big, so I must make sure that the macaroni is heated all the way through and that the cheese is perfectly melted on the top. After twenty minutes, I take a knife and pluck it through the middle: if the knife comes out clean, then it is fully cooked.

Some people like the edge of their macaroni to be a little burnt or dark brown, but I like my edges plain; a little light brown will do, but I prefer the normal look for my macaroni. Once the cheese is melted, the dish is ready to serve and eat.

I learned how to make home-style oven macaroni from my grandmother when I was ten years old, but I wasn't able to cook it on my own until recently. Everyone in my family makes it differently. My auntie's is very good, but she puts Velveeta in hers, which gives it an artificial taste. When I tasted my mom's macaroni, I knew that I wanted to eat it every chance I got. What makes my macaroni stand out is the amount of cheese I use; I put in far more cheese than my mom. I like my macaroni to have an overdose of cheese to the point where you have that long string of cheese as you eat it; I like to call this "the fork effect."

This is why my family and I love my macaroni. As I bite into the cheesy delight, all I can taste is the salty, moist, greasy texture that leaves my taste buds wanting more. Before, I never would have thought that pasta and cheese could taste so good. Making macaroni leaves me feeling both accomplished and satisfied. And while I may think that my macaroni is the best, I still enjoy taste-testing everybody's home-style oven macaroni.

Mingling and Eating

My Saturday Night

IRVING W. FUENTES

It was Saturday night, around eight thirty. My mom and dad and I were getting ready to go out. I took a shower and started getting ready—I put on my pants, shirt, socks, and shoes. After I brushed my teeth, we got in the car and drove to a restaurant called Numero Uno. It wasn't a special night. It was just a regular night, but this was my first time going to that place, so for me it was special. We went through a stop sign—we couldn't see it because it was foggy. But I kept looking out the window even though I couldn't see what was going on outside.

Then we got to the restaurant. When we walked inside, someone took us to the table, and we sat there until the waiter came. While we were waiting, I was looking around at the place: it was calm and cozy like our house. It was a relaxing place, not loud like other restaurants, and the people were very friendly. It made me feel like I was at home. When the waiter came to take our order, we ordered the veggie pizza, with all the vegetables. Then we waited fifteen minutes. In that time, we had a little family chat. We talked about school, my dad's work (which is cool because he's a manager at a construction site), and my mom's day. She said she had fun cleaning the house and was glad to have a night out.

Then our pizza came, and it smelled so good, like I was in heaven. After I looked at the pizza, I covered it with pepper, then put it in my mouth and started chewing. It tasted good and spicy—spicy because of the pepper. The bread was crunchy and soft at the same time, and the cheese tasted good. It was soft and easy to eat, too, not like the cheese at other places like Little Caesars. The vegetables were so good because they were warm and juicy. The taste was amazing. After that, we ate carrot cake, which was good and sweet and delicious.

After we finished eating, we went back to the parking lot. We looked at the car and saw that it had a flat tire. Well, it was medium flat, but we still got in the car and left. After we went to a gas station and put some air in the tire, we headed home safe and sound and happy. When we got to the house, I thought that even though we'd had a flat tire, it had been a pretty good night.

> *My Saturday night*
> *The day we got a flat tire*
> *My first time being in that restaurant*
> *A little chat with the fam bam*
> *What a night*

MEMORABLE DISH

DANAE MEJIA

I woke up on a Saturday morning around eight fifteen because my phone started to ring. It was my lovely sister Emma calling to say she was coming over to my mom's house from the San Fernando Valley. This day is the most memorable day for my mom, sister, and me because I really don't see my sister much. She happens to stay up in the Valley, which takes me about three hours to get to by bus. On the other hand, I also don't see my mom much because she works in Beverly Hills taking care of a ninety-two-year-old man Monday through Saturday. It's like she lives mostly over there.

We walked from Washington and 4th up to Western and Venice, heading to the Food 4 Less. As soon as we walked in, we felt the air conditioning hitting our faces and also smelled the fresh-baked bread. My sister went to get the vegetables while I went in search of the pork. They didn't have little pieces chopped up, so I just got the whole two pounds of meat. Emma went in search of tomatoes, cabbage, onions, lettuce, yuca (cassava), lemon, oil, tortillas, salt, and pepper. Once we had everything, we made it to the long ten- to fifteen-minute checkout line and took out a fifty-dollar bill to pay.

As soon as we got home, I started to wash off the veggies. Afterward, my sister helped me cut them into small pieces a quarter inch across, except for the yuca and lemon. My mom cut up the pork into three-inch-long strips and seasoned it with salt and pepper. When we were finished cutting all the veggies, we added some salt, pepper, and lemon to the minisalad. The yuca had to be cut into four-inch-long pieces and boiled for around ten minutes. The pork was fried over medium heat for ten minutes until we could see it fried up on each side. Finally, we took the pork out of the pan and drained all the oil so we wouldn't have to eat the extra grease.

Happily, everything was almost ready to serve on a big plate and enjoy. We heated up a couple of tortillas per person. We put the yuca on the bottom, added the chopped fried pork on top, and put the salad nicely at the very top. We were happy making this easy meal for all three of us in our little family. This was our mysterious yuca con chicharrón, a delicious Honduran meal.

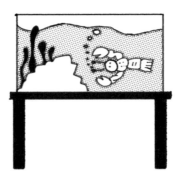

CARNE ASADA WEEKENDS

ELIZABETH GARCIA

One day I was having a good sleep, but suddenly I was awoken by the loud music that my mom was listening to. She told me, "You better wake up because your cousins are coming over." I told her that I didn't want to because I was comfortable sleeping. My mom put the music even louder and louder, so I had to get up and go straight into the shower. Then my mom asked me if I could go with her to the store to buy ranchera meat. I asked, "Are we having carne asada today?" She said yes, and I got excited because my cousins were coming over with my uncles and aunties.

My favorite food is carne asada. I like it with rice, beans, homemade hot sauce, grilled onion, and cheese on top. We usually eat carne asada on weekends. First, I wake up, take a shower, and get ready. When my parents and brother are ready, we go outside, get in the car, and drive to the store. We listen to music or talk in the car. The place we like to buy our meat is called El Poblano, a little minimarket in Huntington Park on Holmes Street. My parents always go there because they say it has better and fresher meat. We park and go inside the store to buy the meat, charcoal, lighter fluid, onions, and peppers. We also buy some chips or soda. Then, we get back in the car, and I start hearing my annoying little brother. He's always crying because my mom never gets him what he wants. On our way to the house he is crying and hitting me because I'm mocking him. After we get out of the car, I help my parents with the stuff we bought.

We go inside, and I start helping my mom prepare the meat. First, I gather the ingredients. Then, I prepare the meat with seasoned salt, orange, and sometimes beer to give the meat some flavor. Meanwhile, my mom and my aunt are cooking the beans and the rice. The way my family cooks the beans, we first put oil in the pan, then fry the beans for five to ten minutes. For the rice, we put oil in the pan and wait two minutes for it to get warm; then we put the rice in to fry and add water. After that, we put in the seasoning and let it cook until the rice is soft.

When I'm done preparing the meat, my dad asks for the meat outside. My mom takes it out and asks my dad and my Uncle Juan if the grill is ready. They say yes, so she puts the meat on the grill. We also like to have grilled onion and grilled nopal (cactus). While we are waiting for the meat to cook, everyone is just talking and laughing. My little brother Jose and my cousin Jasmine are giggling and playing outside. Soon some of the meat is done, so my mom, my Aunt Rosio, and I go inside and start preparing the plates with food. We put rice and beans on the plate, and we get a slice of meat. We take it outside, and my dad and uncle put what they want on top. Usually, we have hot sauce, grilled onion, cheese, and avocado.

While we are eating, I am talking and having a good time with my family. We usually talk about holidays or other stuff. We eat outside in our yard. At my house my yard is pretty big; a lot of people fit in it, so my family always gathers at my house. The rest of my family members either have a small yard, or they live in an apartment. Sometimes we invite other people, and other times we only invite a few of my family members. They usually bring food, so we have a lot to eat.

Carne asada is my favorite food in part because it has a delicious flavor. But mostly, this is my favorite food because I get to spend time with my family—my aunties, uncles, and little cousins. The little kids are so funny. They make me laugh, especially my little brother. He is so cute and helpful, although he can be a scaredy-cat sometimes.

PUPUSAS: WHEN THE WHOLE FAMILY GETS TOGETHER

JOSE WILFREDO MORAN

When I was little and I lived in El Salvador, I used to eat lots of pupusas. When I came to the United States, everything changed. Eating pupusas here is really different from eating them in El Salvador. There are different ways you can eat them. Some people here eat their pupusas with a fork and knife, but that seems too formal. Most of the people who have lived in El Salvador and come to the United States eat them with their hands. Eating with our hands is in our culture. In El Salvador, the times we eat pupusas the most are when the whole family gets together.

One time, we all got together at my grandparents' house. Their house is pretty big with nice colors like baby blue, light green, and lots of other light colors. In El Salvador my parents' families lived close to each other, so one day, we planned for all my cousins, my brother, and me to get together and eat. One of my favorite cousins was named Eduardo, and he loved to joke a lot. He had curly dark brown hair, was kind of dark-skinned, and was a little bit taller than me. He was older than me by six years. Only my older cousins and I got together to eat pupusas on that day. Eduardo made everybody laugh loudly. You could have heard us from across the street. I love when all my cousins and I get together and eat.

My mom was the one making the pupusas for us that day. There are different kinds of pupusas: some of them are made out of cheese, beans, and chicharrón, which is ground pork meat; and there are some with cheese and loroco. Loroco is a type of plant that is mostly grown in El Salvador, and it has a little green flower bud. It tastes sweet and sour, and that's what my mother puts inside the pupusas. There is another type of pupusa made out of rice; the rice flour is different from the corn flour. The pupusas made out of rice flour taste kind of sweet, and they taste really good.

My mom is the only one who really knows how to make pupusas. I love how they taste. I love those days when my mom is in the kitchen cooking them. I love the smell of the cheese melting in the pan and the sound of her hands clapping against the dough. I can hear it all the way across the room. I can feel the heat and smell the taste before they are even done. I can't ever wait until the exact time when my mom shouts, "They are ready!" That's when I run to the dining room and sit at the table with my brother and sister. We see the pile of the pupusas in the center of the table before they all start disappearing one by one.

Eating pupusas here in the United States is really different because you are living in a different culture while trying to fit in with your own culture. I only eat pupusas with my family and sometimes with some friends. Here in the United States, people don't really know what pupusas are or how they taste. The only way they can find out about them is by eating them. We have a different kind of weather here in the United States, and there is not a lot of nature like trees and birds. Here we are, in the middle of a big city, looking out my balcony window eating pupusas.

We had so much fun eating pupusas. Those days are unforgettable; they always come back to my mind. When I think about those days, sometimes they make me happy. Sometimes I get sad because things have changed so much. Hopefully I can have one of those days back because they were so fun. All of the people who have tried my mom's pupusas have said that they taste really good and that they're the best they have ever tried. There are places where you can eat them, but only my mom makes the best pupusas!

The Perfect Pasta

Milan McKinney

Waking up from a long relaxing nap, I smell the burnt scent of my mother pressing her hair with the fire-hot hot comb as she gets ready for my grandfather's birthday dinner party. I get up, shower, put on my favorite little black dress with my perfect little boots, and get ready while thinking about the perfect pasta. My two gremlin sisters are running around the house playing and making a mess as usual. I try to ignore them. It's now 7:15, and the dinner party started at 6:30.

My mother is calmly rushing everyone out of the house as I finish curling the last curl in my bouncy, shiny hair and apply my pretty pink eye shadow. My sisters, my mother, and I speed-walk to the car. Just as we all get buckled up, as if anything else can keep me away from that pasta any longer, my mom says, "Ah shoot, I left my iPhone!" With an irritated look on her face, she runs to the house, impatiently unlocks the door, gets her phone, and then runs back out of the house to the car. As I say, she's overly dramatic. If only the dinner party wasn't so far away; it's nearly in Timbuktu. Okay, maybe I'm exaggerating; thirty-minute drive, max.

While riding in the car, I already know what dish I'm going to order from the Cheesecake Factory: bistro shrimp pasta. It's crisp buttery shrimp, mushrooms (I always order without them), tomatoes, arugula, spaghettini, and lemon-like cream sauce. Oh, my mouth is watering; all the more reason for being extremely impatient with the slow traffic we just ran into.

Finally, after about thirty minutes, with my little sister Katherine annoying me all the way, we arrive at the Grove. Bummer! I wanted to go to the much bigger and nicer Cheesecake Factory in Beverly Hills. Everyone is here at the Grove on a Sunday night; it's kind of crowded. We go into the restaurant, and of course my family is already there. As soon as I walk in, amidst the dim lighting and the sound of dishes hitting against each other, the smell of food hits my nose. We make our way through the crowded lobby to the escalator, and as I get to the top, I spot my family and walk over. My Aunt Shirley gets up, hugs me, and compliments me as usual. (Sometimes she compliments me too much.) I say hello to my family and wish my grandfather a happy birthday. With a big smile on my face, I go and sit next to my favorite cousin, Danny, who always makes me laugh. He gives me a loose one-arm hug and kisses me on the cheek.

Since everyone has already ordered their food, we wait for the waiter to come back. My mom orders just a simple cheese pizza and pink lemonade for my sisters; I order the bistro shrimp pasta, of course, with a shirley temple on the side; and my mom orders the steak diane—Angus beef steak covered with a mushroom wine sauce and served with mashed potatoes and grilled onions. We wait, and they bring us our drinks, but most of all I can't wait for that plate of pasta. I know that I'm not going to be able to finish the whole thing; I never do. Still waiting, I pick at the appetizers and talk to my family. Finally, they bring us our food, and the angels sing from heaven while this golden plate of glowing food comes near and smells so right. I stop talking and just start eating, still listening to everyone's conversation and laughing inside. I've been waiting for this all day, and I finally get it.

Everything was on point: it was my grandfather's birthday that brought us together, I was with my crazy-but-lovely family, and I was having the best dish of my life. The dish itself was not so special; just the pure fact that my family was there increased my pleasure of having it.

I'm moving my plate away and being stingy as my mom tries to pick at my food. I give in and let her taste. I get full and ask the waitress if I can have it to go. She brings me a container, I pack my food, and we stay for a while, just laughing and joking with our family. After about forty minutes, I tell my mom I want to go home. We tell everyone bye, say our last I-love-yous for the night, and walk to the car. Around the third stoplight, I fall asleep thinking about how great my day went with my two most favorite things.

BIG DAY OF COOKING

JANET NAVA

Once upon a time, I met a girl named Rosa at Mount Vernon Middle School. It was my first day going to that school, and my big brother Fernando introduced me to all his very close friends. I was very excited, but at the same time, I was scared because I didn't know them. What if for some reason they just didn't like how I dressed or something like that, and they'd just hate me?

The first person whom my brother introduced me to was Rosa. While I was shaking hands with her, I said my name. She said, "Nice to meet you. Nice name, by they way. I'm Rosa, and you are a pretty young girl. I hope we get along."

And after that, we talked about our schedules so that we could walk together to class, or at least halfway. We did have one class together, and so we walked together. Ever since that day, whenever we had that period, we would walk together to class. And we started to hang around more, too. She is a very nice, cool, and great friend. She is also very wonderful and easy to get along with.

A few months passed. She told me one Monday morning at 8:40, during first period, that I was invited to a little party at her house. She even gave me an invitation; it was kind of a small card with rainbow colors. On the cover it had a picture of her from when she was small and another one that looked like when I met her.

I said, "Oh my God!" because I was really excited and so happy that I got invited to a party. No lie, I had never been invited to some place by an awesome friend like her. She is just really different from the others. It's hard to explain how wonderful she is. I run out of words. She's a friend you wouldn't meet just anywhere.

The day came for my friend's party. I woke up around nine thirty in the morning to make sure that I had everything ready. I was making her favorite food, fiesta chicken enchiladas. I was so excited that I didn't know what to wear for that special day. I went to my closet, and I picked a new dress that I had, one that was not short or long, but in between. It was black with gray, and I matched it with some really high gray heels.

At that time, I didn't know my streets. I looked up her address on some map on my computer and found it. I called her before leaving, and yes, my friend was cool with me coming early to cook. My mom took me to her house, and before going all the way inside, I said, "¡Hola, buenos días!" which means "Hi, good morning" in Spanish. My voice sounded very excited. And after that, I started cooking with her parents' permission; they didn't mind at all.

The ingredients for the dish that I was about to make

were one onion, chopped; one red pepper; one garlic clove, minced; four cooked small chicken breasts, in long shreds; one cup salsa, divided; four ounces light cream cheese (half of an eight-ounce package), cubed; a half cup Kraft Tex-Mex cheese, shredded and divided; and eight six-inch flour tortillas.

It took me about twenty minutes to take all of the ingredients out of the bag and put them in order. I really like to have them in order because then it goes a little faster. And when I started cooking, it took me about forty-five minutes. I tried the first one that I made. It tasted delicious, so spicy and great that I wanted to lick my fingers. That's how good it was.

When I served the food at each table, people just started eating the enchiladas right at that moment. When I saw people eating the food I made, it made me feel so special. I felt so great that day. People were really enjoying it. Also her family members and friends had a great time because out of nowhere we started dancing to bachata and punta (two kinds of Central American/Caribbean music). I was really happy that I was able to make Rosa's favorite meal on a very special day, her birthday.

SOME PEOPLE ASKED FOR MORE

JOSE WILFREDO MORAN

The day of my birthday was very special. I helped cook a kind of Salvadoran food called panes rellenos. I was excited. A pan relleno is bread with chicken and vegetables inside, and it takes a while to get everything ready. This is a really special kind of food you can make for a party or any celebration.

The first thing you need to do is buy the french bread at your favorite bakery. Then you buy the chicken at your favorite market, and you buy the vegetables like cucumber, radish, and cabbage. You need to get everything ready like a salad: you cut the cucumber, the cabbage, and the radish. You then toast the french bread, but not all the way, just a little. You need to wash and get the chicken ready to cook. You put spices on it, and after it is ready, you put it in the oven. When it's ready, you put a special type of salsa on top. Then, you need to cut the chicken in little slices so you can put it in the bread.

You put the chicken inside the bread with the salsa, cucumber, cabbage, and (if you want) the radishes. It's kind of ready, but if you want, you can toast your bread more. Some kids only like their bread with the chicken and no salsa. Some adults might like it with cabbage, cucumber, and radish. You don't have a lot of choices, but you can always make your panes rellenos however you want them.

I asked everyone how they wanted their bread, and I had to try to make it the way they liked it. I was still only learning how to make panes rellenos. I am never going to make them as good as my mom does. (I don't really know how she learned how to cook all these types of foods, but they taste really good. I wish I could learn how to make at least one or two of her dishes.) That day, everybody liked the panes rellenos; some people even asked for more after they finished eating one.

The party was supposedly going to be a surprise, but I found out about it because they made it obvious. I was still surprised because people I don't really speak to came to my party, like my cousin whom I hadn't seen in six years. We spent lots of time having fun, and we played lots of different kinds of music. Everybody was dressed pretty well for my party. I needed to dress really well too because it was my special day. Well, I did; as my brother would say, "You got swag."

My cousins and I had a really good time because it was the only time we could spend together. It was a really special day because all of my family was there with me. It was kind of a small party, but with all the people who were in my house, it seemed like it was pretty big. My parents made my day. I think it was the second-best birthday party I ever had.

1. BOIL THE WATER.

2. ADD SALT.

3. ADD THE NOODLES.

4. DRAIN THE NOODLES.

5. ADD SAUCE AND BUTTER.

6. MIX TOGETHER.

7. FINISHED!

Nice and Juicy

FREDERICK SINGLETON

Few of my friends know how to cook anything. They could ruin cereal. Watching them fumble around the kitchen compared to my cousin Nancy makes me realize what a skill and an art good cooking is. My favorite dish, ground-beef tacos, is not super hard to make, but Nancy puts a lot of love and work into it. She makes them real nice, and if I were to sell my cousin's tacos, I would sell them for ten dollars each. That's how special they really are.

The first food that I ate when I moved in with Nancy was her tacos. About every three or four weeks since, she and I gather food from the grocery store to make these nice, juicy tacos. Nancy is thirty-six, and I've lived with her for some years now. She cooks fried chicken, macaroni and cheese, broccoli and cheese, and steamed vegetables, but my favorite is still the ground-beef tacos. And they are the only thing she makes that we never have left over because they are so tasty that, even if you are full, you still try to get that last bite in.

When we make tacos, we go to the Ralphs on Crenshaw and Jefferson because they have everything we need. We get a basket to put the items in and go to the meat aisle for ground beef, fresh in the package. After that, we go to the seasoning aisle and get taco seasoning—the kind in the red package—to give the tacos a nice flavor. Then we get at least four tomatoes, a head of lettuce, a block of American cheese, and a small container of sour cream (because we don't use a lot of it). The last thing we get is the nice, soft flour taco shells. Now that we are all done shopping, we pay, get into the car, and drive the few blocks home.

To begin, my cousin takes two skillets and puts them on the stove top. She adds olive oil to the skillets and turns the fire up just enough for the meat and shells to cook. After we get everything right where we want it, we take out the cheese, cheese grater, and a bowl, then grate the cheese. We put the ground beef in one skillet over a medium flame and the taco shells in another over a low flame because they both need to be separated and done at the same time. We put some of the cheese on top of the ground beef, and it melts in after a few minutes. The rest of the cheese we set aside.

After the shells are done browning in the skillet, Nancy puts them on a clear glass plate. We grate the rest of the cheese and put it in a bowl, then put the lettuce in a separate bowl. We get two plates from the cabinet; she takes three tacos, and I take four because I eat a lot.

We fill the shells with ground beef, lettuce, tomatoes, cheese, sour cream, and—to top it off—Louisiana hot sauce. Now they are ready to eat. I take some extra cheese and go to the table, which is made of wood with marble squares on it. It's a really tall table—as tall as a bar—and it's really nice to eat on. I'm a clean eater when I eat on it; I do not make a mess when I eat these tacos.

Before the start of 2011, I learned how to make tacos on my own. It was very easy—I had no hard time doing it. I'm really happy that my cousin taught me how to make them. When I made them for her, she said she really liked them and that she taught me well. It was a really good experience to learn how to make them, and it's so easy. I want to have Taco Fridays and start making them every week.

When I'm older and have kids, I will be able to talk about how I learned how to make tacos. I'll pass the recipe down to my kids and their kids, making it a family tradition. Then, when my kids mention tacos, they can make them for me. I can just imagine my kids going to bed and asking me to read the famous story about how I made tacos, the story that made it into this book.

JUST TO SEE A SMILE

YUISI DENNIS

A couple of days before my birthday, thoughts are in the air of what I want to do. I'm turning seventeen; I'm getting older; I'm almost an adult. I'm excited to choose where to eat for my birthday. Should I go fancy like Castaway, or should I come in under the budget and go to Porto's Bakery? Porto's hits my taste buds when I hear the bakery's name coming from my mom and sister. Looking back to the humor, cheerful times, and endless smiles at Porto's, I feel it would be great to go there for my birthday. Even though I wanted to go fancy for once, nothing can beat the smiles of my loved ones.

I am filled with excitement even though we've been to Porto's many times. Money has been an issue lately, so whatever money is spent on me to have a great birthday, I'm going to appreciate. It's also an opportunity to eat great pastries, a well-seasoned tuna croissant, and—to top it off—a fruit tart bordered with whipped cream and sprinkled with granola bits.

As I wait for my birthday, my stomach grows anxious. I want to fast the last day so that I can enjoy one great afternoon meal. Lying down in bed the night before my birthday, my anxiety grows, knowing exactly what I'm going to order although all I really want is jubilant smiles from my siblings and, especially, my mother. I go to sleep, and it seems that in no time I'm awake, ready to start the next day.

In the morning, the first to surprise me is my girlfriend, with a desk lamp that I need. Soon after, my little brother wakes up and gives me my birthday hugs. As we head to school, my girlfriend brightens up my day. And when I get to school, friends give me hugs. I say to myself, *My day has started out good.*

After every period my stomach grumbles more and more. It tenses up. I don't even have a six-pack, but it feels like all my stomach muscles were flexing into eight. Getting near the end of school, all I can imagine is my cake topped with fruits of all vibrant colors. I'm hoping for it but doubting I'll get it at the same time.

I come out of school with a Kool-Aid smile, like when I was in grade school and winter or summer vacation came along. My mom is quick to call me.

"¿Ya vienes? Are you coming already?" she asks.

Walking home from school, I come across fast-food restaurants and barbecue shops that make my stomach ache. Tempted to buy a drink, I wait, hold my patience, and keep walking, ignoring juicy burger advertisements and pictures of creamy Burger King vanilla shakes that are good for a summer day, but not today. Today all I want is my tuna sandwich and fruit tart. Once I get to Norton Avenue, anxiety grows at the thought of potato balls filled with ground beef and cheese. My mouth is quick to salivate like a starving dog's.

As I walk into my house, the first thing I see is the colorful fruit tart sitting in the middle of the table. *I can't wait to grab a couple slices,* I say to myself. I head to my room to drop off my backpack and empty my pockets. I have a minor headache from a long day at school, nothing big. Then I go outside and feed my dogs—a pit bull mix and Akita mix. Happy to see me, they jump on me and get me dirty, so I have to change. Soon after, I rush to the table eager to eat, hungry from a long day at school.

After receiving hugs and good wishes from everyone in my family, the feasting begins. I enjoy taking my first bite into the fresh tuna sandwich, then grabbing a hot yellow chili pepper that turns my lips red. I bite again after a sip of ice-cold Dr. Pepper. Halfway through my tuna sandwich, I grab a potato ball—seasoned beef and pork, covered by potato and bread crumbs, then lightly fried. I put a little bit of Tapatio to add a bit of spice.

Once the fruit tart starts getting cut, my little brother is quick to grab the birthday-boy slice. I let him, knowing he had a long day at school, too. I grab a slice, tasting every flavor of the kiwi, watermelon, pineapple, sweet-and-sour apple, coconut, mango, and my favorite—strawberry. Every color of fruit combines into a rainbow. The acidic taste flows through my mouth. It feels like with every bite I take, I go into a hole and count down every childhood year. I know to appreciate what I get because I may not have the same people around me in the future.

Things are things. You can spend time on things, or with your loved ones, I think to myself.

After enjoying every last bit of the first slice, I grab one more. It is a great-tasting fruit tart. My mom and sister, along with my girlfriend, are making jokes about how much I was craving my fruit tart and how I finally had it. A "woman trio," I call them. I tell myself that I am going to get a third slice—it is just so irresistible. When I finish eating, my stomach is crammed with great flavors. I am satisfied and happy. We don't finish the tart, so that means I have more to stuff my face with later.

The whole day went how I pictured it: no arguments and a great afternoon meal with my family. The day couldn't have gone better. I was embraced by love, by what my family did for me just to see a smile on my face.

Time flies. Age is just a number. Growing comes with knowledge, wisdom, and experience. I didn't feel seventeen. I don't know what age I felt, but I did know that I was still a kid, growing older by the second.

Out of a Few Simple Ingredients

Luther Meriweather

It's a calm afternoon, and I'm about to watch the Eagles vs. Cardinals game with my cousin Josh. As I take a seat in the living room to watch the game, Josh tells me to get him a chair, cutting board, tomatoes, jalapeños, habaneros, onions, and a bottle of taco sauce. I just give him a look that says, *Man, I just sat down.*

Josh and I had just come from Food 4 Less with groceries, so I knew that he wanted to make chicken tacos. My cousin is the type of person who will go to the store and stay longer than expected—it can be annoying at times, but I've learned to deal with it.

At the store, we had walked around looking for what he needed to make the tacos. We found the ingredients, paid for them, and then went home to prepare the food.

Now, as I gather up these foods, I take a second to stop

and stare at them. I find it amazing how Josh uses his creative mind to make such a delicious topping out of a few simple ingredients. I set up the board so that he can start chopping the vegetables.

In the kitchen, I take the chicken out of the refrigerator and grab the rice from the cabinet. I clean the chicken thoroughly and put it in a pot of water on the stove, and then I put some rice in another pot. As I leave it there to boil, I go into the living room to see how Josh is doing with the ingredients. It hasn't even been a minute, but he is already finishing cutting up the tomatoes, habaneros, and onions. All that is left is the jalapeños—he finishes them, dumping the peppers into the bowl with everything else.

Once he finishes, we both go into the kitchen to check on the chicken and rice. I use a spoon to stir the rice so that it doesn't get stuck to the pot. Josh uses a fork to check if the chicken is tender. After a few minutes, the chicken seems tender enough, so I get a plate and start shredding the meat. While I do that, my cousin gets some seasoning from the kitchen drawer to mix with the chicken. When I finish shredding the chicken, my cousin mixes up the rice with the meat and seasons it. The mixture has a funny smell, but it looks good enough to eat.

Once everything is ready, all that's left to do is cook the tortillas. I grab a pan, pour some cooking oil in it, and put it on top of the stove. I turn on the stove and wait for the oil to get hot so I can lay the tortillas into it. One by one, as I lay each tortilla in the pan, folding them into the shape of the moon, I am reminded why I love making tacos. It's not the food that I love so much, nor is it being in the kitchen helping my cousin. It's the way preparing this food makes my family bonds stronger and stronger. I guess you could say that food brings our family closer together. I guess love has its funny ways of working.

My Mother's Catch Phrase

Brian Young

It was a midsummer night, but we all were nicely chilled thanks to the AC. That night was special because my mom was making her homemade Brandon family, ultra-secret recipe, Saint Louis–style gumbo. Everyone's mouths watered, and stomachs roared in anticipation of the meal to come. Whenever my mom made gumbo, we would skip meals that day just to make sure we could eat our fill…and then some.

We all had to help prepare the ingredients for the meal. Byran and I sat at the living room table cleaning the shrimp. We always cleaned the shrimp, even though neither of us liked to do it. Our hands would go numb from handling the frigid shrimp, and we didn't like the fishy stench that all seafood seems to have before it's cooked. Still, Byran and I considered it a trivial chore and were more than happy to do it if it meant we were going to get a hearty helping of gumbo. Brandon leaned up against the kitchen counter as he rolled the chicken in flour and dropped it in a massive skillet of boiling vegetable oil. As the chicken fell into the oil, it popped and crackled. The aroma coming from the kitchen danced around the house and nearly drove us crazy. Angela plopped down on the sofa, switched on the TV, and began chopping Farmer John sausage links; the sound of her knife repeatedly striking the plate annoyed me to no end. It reminded me of the sound of a baby banging a cup against the floor. My mom was in the kitchen preparing the rice, king crab legs, and the monstrous pot that she would later use to combine everything in. The pot was so large that we had to remove two racks from the fridge in order to store it. Brandy, the youngest member of our family, was stuck doing the odd jobs: throwing things away, cleaning up spills, getting paper towels, etc. She must have really been irritated by our commands.

After everything was prepared, we took the ingredients into the kitchen and stepped back to let my mother work. The ingredients were her paints, and the pot was her canvas: a dash of rust-colored seasoned salt, a bit of ebony pepper. The rest of her colors are sacred knowledge that I am forbidden to learn. Then we did the only thing we could do, wait.

The hands on the clock seemed to move at the same speed as tectonic plates. We all ventured off to find something to distract ourselves from our growing stomach pains. Byran and I went into my room and began a long campaign of *Star Wars: Battlefront II*. Byran played as one of the soldiers on the front line, and I was a sniper watching his back. After a while, we heard a ruckus coming from the living room, so we put the game on pause and went to investigate. It came from Brandon and Angela, who were locked in another one of their periodic arguments. First they were lovey-dovey. Then they would argue over some trivial matter. They were fighting—playfully, of course. After that they went back to being lovey-dovey. (It was always an amusing-but-bizarre spectacle. I often joke about recording them and posting the video on YouTube.) After Brandon and Angela settled down, I sat on the arm of the couch. That's when I noticed Brandy trying to help Mama in the kitchen. She mostly got in the way, but she tried. I watched her for a little while longer; she looked like she was studying our mother. Maybe she was preparing for the day she would make gumbo with her own family.

After an eon of waiting, my mom finally uttered those words we had been craving to hear: "*Y'all can eat!*" It was her catch phrase, something we never tired of hearing.

Once she said her line, we rushed to the bathroom to wash our hands and then bolted to the kitchen. We all began to move in a ritualistic pattern: grab a bowl, put rice at the bottom, scoop a mountain of gumbo on top of it, grab a drink, and sit down. Soon the sounds of king crab legs being snapped open, spoons slapping the insides of bowls, sodas being sipped, napkins wiping mouths, *mmmm*ing, and the scraping of that last corner of gumbo (which always tasted the best) glided through the house. If anyone saw us, they would think we hadn't eaten for weeks.

After the meal, everyone retreated to their rooms to climb

into their beds. Tired, sleepy, satisfied, and completely resistant to movement, everyone fell asleep, one after another… everyone except me. Unfortunately it was my day to clean the dishes. I dragged my full, heavy, and comfortably warm body into the kitchen; for about five minutes I stared at the tower of dirty dishes that had accumulated. Then I turned around, leaving the leaning tower undisturbed. I lumbered into my room and eased into my bed. I knew my mother would probably yell at me in the morning and tack on another day of dish duty, but at that moment I couldn't care less. I was too full to stay awake. I grabbed my MP3 player and listened to "Aqueous Transmission" by Incubus. To this day I don't think I've heard another song with such a beautiful, relaxing, peaceful, and trance-inducing melody. As I lay in my bed I thought of "Aqueous Transmission" and how it's a mix of Western and Eastern cultures; how the gumbo is a mix of meat, poultry, and seafood; and how Mama, Brandon, Byran, Brandy, Angela, and I all come together and make this misfit family. More importantly, it made me think about how peaceful that night was. Peace never lasted long in this house. It was best to enjoy it while we could.

Almost every day, students, parents, educators, and policy makers weather a storm about academic achievement versus academic failure. Rarely does this discussion rest on anything other than test scores. Have we accepted the idea that success can be found only within the confines of a test-form bubble?

I hope this book project can serve as a reminder that learning is meant to burst through the seams and sneak through the lines. Often, when a student succeeds, it's believed to be because of some miraculous teacher who has a special gift. As a teacher with several teaching awards, I can confidently say the success of my students is *not* mine. It belongs to multiple people and multiple organizations. It belongs to parents and teachers, to the organizations that support them, and—most importantly—it belongs to the students. Learning is a community endeavor, and when it works best, it is shared among many. Without Jane Patterson and the amazing team at Los Angeles Education Partnership, my students would never have met Joel Arquillos, Julius Diaz Panoriñgan, and the remarkable team at 826LA who donated the resources and the time to make this book possible. And, without 826LA, we would never have been able to work with the artists at Yello,Friends!, who have made this book look so amazing. Without people like Stacey Vigallon, the curriculum for this book would never have been written, and the work would have not been as rich. Thanks to these organizations and individuals, Alice Waters donated her time and unique perspective to add context to the student content of this book. All of these members help create a vibrant community of learning for students. All of the above people deserve recognition for helping push this project to completion.

Many years ago, my mentor, Tom Gage, taught me about the importance of community in education. This project—especially the way a diverse community of professionals, students, families, and educators collaborated—helped me understand how community makes learning possible.

Robert Jeffers

Dorsey High School

Aside from being five foot two and one hundred ten pounds, **Jamise Caesar** is a student of diverse interests: Mandarin, film, and Yosemite. Even though she's only seventeen, she is the oldest seventeen-year-old you'll ever meet.

Jalisa "Juju" Miller is a hyped-up sixteen-year-old who is high on nothing but life itself. A Los Angeles native, she's a goofy and playful person who always has a smile on her face. She participates in as many activities as she can at Dorsey: softball, football, golf, drill team, eco club, and band.

Kendra Glover is the queen of mash-ups. You can always catch her with a snack; if she doesn't have her snacks, you know something's wrong.

Danae Mejia attends Dorsey High and has sadly celebrated her birthday on September 11 since 1993. A quiet girl, Danae always does her work on time, especially for APUSH (AP United States History). She has a part-time job at Charley's Steakery at the Baldwin Hill Crenshaw Plaza, and she hopes to attend UCLA after graduation.

Joyce Realegeno was born January 18 to hardworking Salvadoran parents. She is passionate about animal science. She turned to a vegetarian diet in the eighth grade, studied corvids as part of an internship, and coordinated a bird count. In the future, she plans to major in Wildlife Science. When Joyce looks back on her high school years, she'll remember habitat restoration projects and her love for Ronnie James Dio.

Rika R. Thibodeaux loves going camping and hiking. At home, she eats whatever she can get her hands on. She reads books constantly and loves laughing and hanging out with her friends. To stay awake for sixth period, she fills up on candy.

Brian Young loves fantasy stories and also writes them. He plays both the guitar and the flute, and hopes to one day open his own animation/video game/ music studio. He considers himself a nerd who likes to have fun.

At Dorsey, we students are all about food and thank-yous. Though we may not always say things the right way, we hope you know what we mean.

Thank you, first, to our parents for allowing us to contribute to this project, for putting up with late-night writing, and for providing us with food. (A special thanks to Brian's mom for the deliciously amazing wonder-gumbo. It was sooo good! And Jamise—there was rice.)

To all at 826LA, thank you for this opportunity. To the tutors, thanks for the help with our drafts. To Neekta, Mary, and Lauren: thanks for putting up with our shenanigans, and thanks for bringing us all the snacks from Trader Joe's. You guys are awesome! And Julius, many thanks for all the fun and hard work, and for keeping us focused. (You are really funny, by the way.)

We are incredibly appreciative of the City of Los Angeles for the diversity of its food in restaurants like Jack in the Box, Grandma Lucia's, Porto's, and Ocha. Thanks to everyone who comes to our houses and eats our food, and thanks also to the freeload victims who are kind enough to share their food and put up with our presence.

To our fellow students, thanks for putting in the time and effort needed to make this book happen. (Kendra: thanks for Freeloaderism and mash-ups.) Dr. Sample, thank you for your support. Miss Stacey, thank you for sharing your sweet drawing skills and all those lessons on art. Alice Waters, thank you so much for writing the foreword to our book. Yello,Friends!: you have amazing creativity; thank you for the great art that graces this book's pages. There would be no book without you.

To Mr. Jeffers, our teacher: words can't explain how thankful we are for you and everything you do for us. Thanks for the angry where-are-you texts, and the looks you give us in the hallway when we "forget" about meetings. More importantly, thanks for giving us opportunities to grow and learn, and for helping create a path to a brighter future. You truly are the teacher who does it all.

And finally, thanks to all of you for reading this book.

Martha L. Andrade is a tenth-grade student at Dorsey High School.

Jesus Aquino, a sixteen-year-old sophomore, enjoys swimming, practicing his guitar, and listening to music. He is a friendly person who enjoys the company of his friends. He visited Texas once. He also likes to draw, even though he isn't all that good at it.

Taylor Broom, a student at Dorsey High School for all four years, is excited to graduate in June 2011. After high school, Taylor wants to pursue a career as a family nurse practitioner. Taylor's utopia would be a two-story house, three cars, three kids, a husband, and her BFF Jasmine Littlejohn.

Gary Paul Burbridge was born on Mother's Day in Long Beach, and he now lives in Los Angeles. He is thought of as an overachiever.

Olga DeLeTorre loves spending time with friends and family. She enjoys taking trips with her family, including traveling to Mexico every December. She loves watching her brother play soccer and the color purple.

Yuisi Dennis was born and raised in the Crenshaw district of Los Angeles, about twelve miles from the Pacific coast. He is a swimmer, now a senior at Dorsey High School. He looks forward to enduring new experiences, learning, and expanding his horizons. He loves painting, drawing, building, sculpting, and writing. He enjoys passing his time with his dogs and reestablishing the California environment.

Alysa R. Drew is an athletic person, a dancer, and fashionista.

Marcos Durán was born and raised in Inglewood, and is now a tenth grader at Dorsey High. His favorite subject is math because it is easy, and his least favorite subject is English because sometimes it gets too hard. Marcos has two brothers and one sister.

Dana Flores was born and raised in Los Angeles. Her favorite

sport is soccer. She loves going out with her friends, having fun, and playing soccer on Saturdays.

Jessica Azucena Alberto Franco is a tenth-grade student at Dorsey High School.

Irving W. Fuentes is a tenth-grade student at Dorsey High School.

Angie Lilibeth Garcia is a tenth-grade student at Dorsey High School.

Elizabeth Garcia was born in Los Angeles. A tenth grader at Dorsey High, she likes to hang out with friends and travel. She loves going to Mexico; she goes there every summer.

Helen Elizabeth Garcia, sixteen years old, was born and raised in LA by her parents, who are both from El Salvador. She comes from a big family and loves music, reading, and writing little stories. She and her brother were born on the same day, February 15, but in different years.

Larnell Grant, an African American student at Dorsey

High, has lived with his grandma since he was two years old. He loves rap, R&B, and rock music, and especially likes to listen to the rapper Tupac and the singer Dan Black. A fan of horror movies and acting out movie roles, his favorite movie character is Freddy Krueger from *A Nightmare on Elm Street.*

Micheliza Hernandez, a native of Los Angeles, plays both guitar and bass, but prefers the bass. She likes punk music and dying her hair different colors. Unsure of what the future

brings, she likes to live in the moment.

Steven Lawton is a cheerleader and a dancer. He is outgoing, outspoken, loud, and fun to be around. His favorite color is red. A lover of fashion, Steven has a different bag to match his outfit every day.

Priscilla Lira is a tenth-grade student at Dorsey High School.

Jasmine Littlejohn is a senior at Dorsey High School. She loves to laugh, enjoys quiet time and BlackBerry Messenger, and looks happily forward to a future of college, working, and handling more challenging responsibilities. Jazy loves her life, she might say.

Milan McKinney is a unique and artsy person who loves fashion and music, especially indie

rock, rap, R&B, and hip-hop. She enjoys Facebook and spending time with her friends. Her number-one inspiration is Rihanna, for both her music and her style. Milan hopes to attend New York University and major in either fashion or photography.

Luther Lawrence Meriweather IV was born on May 13 and raised by his grandparents. At Dorsey High School, he met his true friend, Monica Aguirre. They started out their lives in high school as confused freshmen and are ending it as studious seniors. Luther has been through a lot but still manages to keep a sane brain. Next year, he will be attending Northridge along with his best friend, Monica.

Marresha Milner is a young lady of sixteen, currently a junior at Dorsey High School. She grew up in California and was brought up by a good family. She has many hopes, dreams, and goals. She maintains a 3.2 GPA and is on the honor roll. She wants to attend UC Santa Barbara and study to become a pediatrician.

Gabriel Montoya is a tenth grader who is into wrestling. He's a restoration leader with Los Angeles Audubon.

Jose Wilfredo Moran, a tenth grader at Dorsey High, likes to play soccer and hang out with his friends. He is a friendly and trustworthy person who loves to eat pupusas. He is very talented and smart.

Janet Nava likes to hang out with her best friend Selen Mateo. She is a friendly person who is easy to get along with and who likes to enjoy life. She loves to dance and calls it her main theme. She also enjoys shopping and partying.

Stephanie Overton was born in Erie, Pennsylvania, and now lives in Los Angeles. She loves to watch sports. Currently, her two favorite sports teams are the Los Angeles Lakers and the Philadelphia Eagles. In order to pursue a nursing career, Stephanie hopes to attend Prairie View University. Her favorite colors are sky blue, purple, pink, and yellow.

Symone Owens is a senior. She runs track, loves Thai food, and is a fan of suspense movies.

Isaira Padilla is a twelfth-grade student at Dorsey High School.

Ernesto Rigoberto Panameno was born in El Salvador in 1994 and came to the United States in 2002. He attended Virginia Road Elementary School and Mount Vernon Middle School before attending Dorsey High School. Ernesto, a practicing Christian, dreams of becoming a math or science teacher.

Blanca Reyes loves eating, sleeping, exploring, and living life. She is a happy person who enjoys challenges, being outside, and camping with family and friends. She feels blessed to have her family, and she spends her extra time playing with her dog, Happy.

Ivanna Rodriguez is an eleventh-grade student at Dorsey High School.

Kevin Ruiz, an outgoing tenth grader at Dorsey High, loves to draw. He also likes games, music, sports, making friends, eating, and learning new things. His favorite subjects are English and science.

Frederick Singleton is an eleventh-grade student at Dorsey High School.

Aleah Smith lives in Los Angeles, where she is an exemplary student and a wonderful person to be around. She enjoys camping, biking, hanging out with friends, and eating. She also plays on the softball team.

Sharnise Turner was born in Inglewood, lived in the Moreno Valley, and now resides in Los Angeles. A sunny, outgoing, and caring person, she plans to make something positive out of her life.

Engelle Valenzuela
was born and raised in
Los Angeles. A senior
at Dorsey High, she has
run both cross-country
and track since the
ninth grade. Her future
career goals include
acting and writing.

Raymond Villanueva
was born in Bakersfield
and now lives in Los
Angeles with his three
siblings and his parents.
He enjoys listening
to all kinds of music,
playing video games,
and drawing. Raymond
is a senior.

And now, a toast.

Like the student editorial board, we hope you've enjoyed this smorgasbord of stories. We also hope you return for seconds and thirds and more. That is the magic of *From the Couch to the Kitchen*, the potential to relive our beautifully ephemeral experiences with food—the hunger and longing, the intimacy of cooking, the joy of finally eating. At 826LA, we like to talk about the long lifespan of our books, and we cannot do this without pointing out the effort that goes into preparing them for publication.

It's not just effort. For us, this book is like Aleah's mom's steak and cheesy broccoli, or Brian's mom's gumbo (which we've had the pleasure of trying)—a labor of love. The publication process is long and never without its little spills (both literal and metaphorical) and kitchen fires (thankfully, just metaphorical); but ultimately, we consider ourselves fortunate to pour so much of ourselves, alongside so many others, into a book for all of you.

Thanks to all at Dorsey High School who have supported this project: Dr. Reginald Sample, the principal; administrators Barbara Chanaiwa and Lorraine Machado; and teachers Mary Clare Freeman, Xioali Kelly, Carolyn Libuser, Tessa Main, Donald Singleton, Jamal Speakes, and David Wu. Thanks also to Stacey Vigallon, honorary member of the Dorsey family, for all you do for these students, notably the art instruction that led to many of the sketches and illustrations in this book. Most of all, thanks to Robert Jeffers, the teacher at the center of this partnership. Robert has been at work on this book for longer than anyone at 826LA: we first came to his classroom last November, but the project grew out of a food-based curriculum he implemented last school year. Thanks, Robert, for welcoming us into your classrooms, and more importantly, thank you for your 'round-the-clock devotion to your students. You say you sleep (some), but we're not sure we believe you.

To the young authors: we won't forget the hundreds of cries of "I'm so hungry!" that echoed throughout Mr. Jeffers' classroom from our very first visit. Even before you set pen to paper, your words had power. You've grown so much, and your writing has come so far. Along with countless others, we'll now think of you when we enjoy some Jack in the Box or PB and apples, or when we try to make jaiba or macaroni and cheese. Thanks for making us hungry, and thanks for keeping us satisfied.

This book would not be here without the invaluable support of many of 826LA's volunteers. First and most important here are the volunteers who came to Dorsey High School to assist with revision after revision for almost three months: Lee Carroll, Elisha Cohn, Lisa Fetchko, Lauren Gravitz, Mary Guterson, Kaya Haig, Aly Iwamoto, Clea Litewka, Will Richter, Danielle Roderick, Athena Schindelheim, Regina Stagg, J. Ryan Stradal, Marie Weiss, and Helen Zhao. Thank you all.

After the in-school portion of the project finished, work began on editing the student work. Lisa Fetchko, Lauren Gravitz, Mary Guterson, Aly Iwamoto, and Regina Stagg followed up their work in the classroom with editing support, and they were joined by Robert Bravo, Melissa Crowley, Barbara Dobkin, Amy Dunkleberger, Saku Ee, Lilly Fowler, Russ Frazier, Barbara Galletly, Liriel Higa, Constance Hsiao, Gia Hughes, Camille Knox, Summer Block Kumar, Diana McCrimmon, Kirstin McLatchie, Tania Mirza, Mindy Nguyen, Louise Nutt, Eileen Roggin, Anna Roth, Liz Ruff, Indu Bulbul Sanwal, Jacob Savage, Michelle Snyder, Natasha Stephan, Stephanie Strauss, Katie Thomason, Jessica Tong, Jade Tran, and Emily Twombly. We couldn't have done this without your tireless work. Gia and Mary in particular deserve special recognition for their swift edits and later-night responses to late-night emails.

We now must express our gratitude for a handful of essential volunteers. Among 826LA's most dedicated volunteers are its interns, who support everything we do, including our publications. Thank you to Durdana Karim, Neekta Khorsand, Rachel Leddy, Kelley Lonergan, Nate Mayer, Samantha Moeller, Julene Paul, Bianca Pinedo, Amanda Skeels, Eric Stolze, and Bobby Wilson for tutoring, editing, and helping us manage all the littlest details. We again applaud Lauren Gravitz, Mary Guterson, and Neekta Khorsand, this time for acting as insightful, sure-handed advisors to the student editorial board. To the Yello,Friends! design team—Pei-Jeane Chen, Patrick Leung, Carlo Llacar, and Saejean Oh—this book is so beautiful thanks to you. This is the most elegant, intricate book design we've ever had, and we'll count ourselves lucky if we get to do this together again. And to Alice Waters (along with everyone at Chez Panisse, especially Cristina Mueller)—thanks for sharing your reflective words in the foreword, and for inspiring all involved with this project.

We cannot forget to acknowledge the Goldhirsh Foundation and its continued support of young authors and 826LA publications. Your gift funded the production of this book, and enabled us to get off the couch and produce this literary feast. Thank you, yet again, so much.

Last, but certainly not least, we are so grateful for the opportunity we've had to work with the student editorial board: Jamise Caesar, Kendra Glover, Danae Mejia, Jalisa Miller, Joyce Realegeno, Rika Thibodeaux, and Brian Young. Your writing is some of the funniest and most touching in this book, and yet that's the least of your contributions. Starting with just a stack of submitted drafts, you ultimately decided what this book would be: you organized chapters, helped direct design, wrote extra material, and gave this book a name. We've lost track of how many hours we've spent in the kitchen with you, and we're sad to see this phase of our journey end. We can't wait for the potluck, though, and beyond.

We are Yello,Friends!

A group of visual chefs armed
with sporks and laptops.
We snack incessantly while
designing books and making
other delicious things. We dwell
in Los Angeles (better known as
the food capital of the known
universe) and enjoy eating
eggs, Nilla wafers, sushi, and
pistachio ice cream.

From the Couch to the Kitchen
is our second project with
826LA. Our first was *If I Tell
You*, a collection of the best
stories from 2009 to 2010.

www.yellofriends.com
www.twitter.com/yellofriends

COLOPHON

This first-edition book is set in 11 pt. Sabon, with headlines set in Base Nine. Spot illustrations were based on original student artwork and were redrawn by Patrick Leung and Saejean Oh. Cover and book design by Pei-Jeane Chen and Carlo Llacar. Printed in Minnesota by Bang Printing, April 2011.

A NON-PROFIT WRITING & TUTORING CENTER

About 826LA

826LA is a nonprofit organization dedicated to supporting students ages 6 to 18 with their creative and expository writing skills, and to helping teachers inspire their students to write. We believe that strong writing skills are fundamental to future success, and, with this in mind, we provide challenging and enjoyable programs, all of them free, that ultimately strengthen each student's power to express ideas effectively, creatively, confidently, and in his or her individual voice.

After-School Tutoring Our method is simple: our tutors provide students with one-on-one help. It is our understanding that, with concentrated help from knowledgeable tutor-mentors, students can make great leaps in English skills and comprehension within hours.

Workshops We offer writing workshops taught by professional artists and our talented volunteers. From comic books to screenplays, bookmaking to radio, our wide variety of workshops is perfect for passionate young writers.

In-School Projects Our extensive volunteer base allows us to partner with many schools in Los Angeles. We send volunteers out to support teachers in their classrooms by providing one-on-one tutoring on assignments ranging from fractured fairy tales to college essays.

Field Trips We want to help Los Angeles teachers get their students excited about writing while helping students to better express their ideas, so we welcome classes for field trips during the school day. Our most popular field trip is Storytelling & Bookmaking; the entire class works with our tutors to create a story with illustrations, which is made into a book for each student to take home.

826LA.org
info@826LA.org